THE CULTURAL TRIANGLE OF SRI LANKA

Sri Lanka is a country that has fascinated the world with our eons old civilisation, heritage, culture and history. We are a proud nation of the Lion People that have been strengthened by the dreams of our forefathers. Likewise, Durdans is a truly Sri Lankan hospital with an inherent history and culture that carries the dream of a healthy Sri Lankan nation on its shoulders.

Having always been aware of being a socially responsible corporate citizen, in celebrating our 60th anniversary, we have focused on the re-conservation of the historic Mihintale Hospital (Vedahala) to give back to our country some of the heritage we have lost with time. In similar vein, through the proceeds of this volume produced by the Central Cultural Fund and UNESCO, we will contribute towards the re-conservation of the country's heritage, bringing about a renaissance to Sri Lanka's ancient historical sites.

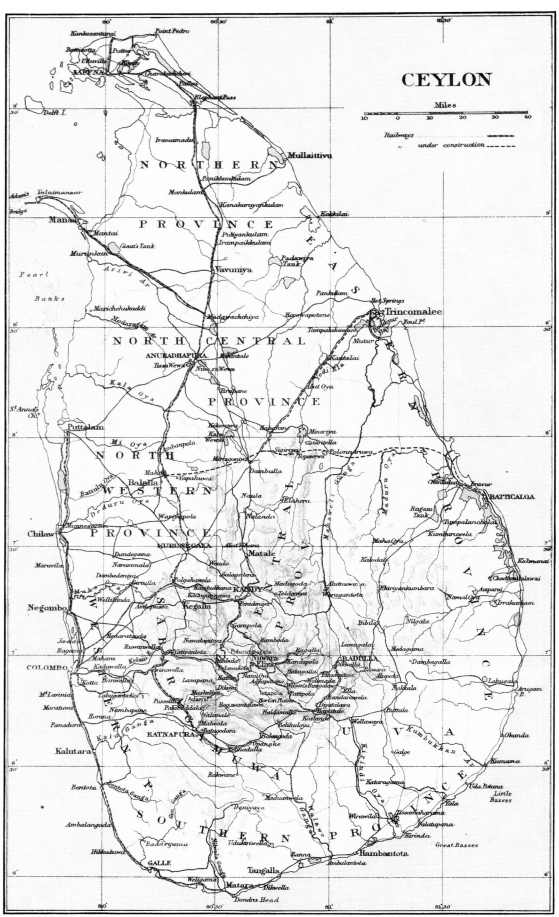

CEYLON

Miles

Railways
„ under construction

London. John Murray.

THE CULTURAL TRIANGLE
OF SRI LANKA

UNESCO PUBLISHING / CCF

First Print 1993
Second Print 1995
Third Print 2001
Fourth Print 2002
Fifth Print 2004
Sixth Print 2005

First published in 1993 by the United Nations Educational, Scientific and Cultural Organization
7, Place de Fontenoy
75700 Paris, France

and

Central Cultural Fund (CCF)
Ministry of Cultural Affairs and Information
Colombo 7, Sri Lanka

Design: Albert Dharmasiri / Barry Lane
Cover : Jean – Francis Chériez, UNESCO Publishing
Frontispiece : Map of Ceylon (Sri Lanka),
        G. E. Mitton, 1916.

Printed by Aitken Spence Printing (Pte) Ltd.
Colombo 13, Sri Lanka.
Typeset by Lazerprint, Colombo 3, Sri Lanka.

ISBN (UNESCO) 92-3-102874-X
ISBN (CCF) 955-613-046-2

Foreword

by His Excellency D. B. Wijetunga,
President of Sri Lanka

Few countries have maintained an unbroken record of their political, religious and cultural history for over twenty-five centuries with such accuracy and detail as Sri Lanka has done. It is equally significant that this long historical record is corroborated by independent evidence from inscriptions, artifacts and monuments. It is also supported by literary evidence from Chinese, Greek, Latin and Sanskrit sources and epigraphical data from India, Indonesia, Myanmar and Thailand. Furthermore, Sri Lanka has developed and preserved its pluralistic religious, linguistic and literary heritage down through the ages. In doing so it has distinguished itself and rendered great service to humanity as a testimony to the multi-faceted splendour of human achievement.

It is in recognition of the exceptional universal value of the Sri Lankan cultural heritage that the Ministers of Education and Economic Development recommended to UNESCO in 1978 that it had a major task to undertake in Sri Lanka. It was stressed that the cultural achievements of Sri Lanka belonged to humanity as a whole and had therefore to be safeguarded as a global obligation to generations yet unborn.

Six exceptional sites in a triangular area bounded by Anuradhapura, Polonnaruva and Kandy were identified for special attention and the project was appropriately called 'The Cultural Triangle of Sri Lanka'. The General Conference of UNESCO in October 1978 approved the project which was assigned the same status as the remarkable international efforts to save Abu Simbel, Borobodur, Moenjodaro and Venice.

An international campaign was launched by the then Director-General of UNESCO, Mr Amadou Mahtar M'Bow, in the historic Audience Hall of Kandy on 25 August 1980. The master plan was finalized and signed by UNESCO and the Government of Sri Lanka in December 1980. The overriding priority which the Government of Sri Lanka has assigned to this project is most eloquently exemplified by the fact that the Central Cultural Fund, set up for the purpose, was administered by a Board of Governors with the Prime Minister as *ex-officio* Chairman.

His Excellency President Ranasinghe Premadasa chaired the Board for ten years and personally directed every aspect of the work. It should be gratefully recorded that his singular commitment and personal involvement laid a lasting foundation to the enormous accomplishments of the project during the first decade.

When Mr Federico Mayor, Director-General of UNESCO, visited Sri Lanka to celebrate the tenth anniversary of the Cultural Triangle Project, Sri Lanka could proudly present to him a series of outstanding achievements ranging from breathtaking discoveries and landmarks in conservation to the formation of no less than two hundred highly skilled specialists in archaeological excavation and conservation. I am myself privileged to have served as Chairman of the Board of Governors of the Central Cultural Fund over the last four years.

The international recognition not only of the importance of the Cultural Triangle but also of the magnitude of the work accomplished was expressed in tangible form when the General Conference of UNESCO in 1991 identified the Sri Lanka Project as one of the four international campaigns to be made the focus of intensive action during the current biennium. It is significant that the Cultural Triangle is the only project of its kind outside Africa and the Arab States.

This beautiful volume with its comprehensive account of each of the sites and a wealth of illustrations is appearing in compliance with UNESCO's decision to renew the call it made in 1980 to its Members States to participate in the project. It specifically draws the attention of the international community to the tasks yet to be accomplished and solicits its involvement and cooperation.

Sri Lanka is grateful for the generous support that it has received from such intergovernmental agencies as the World Food Programme and the United Nations Development Programme and from Britain, China, Japan and many other friendly countries. Every visitor to Sri Lanka has voluntarily become a partner through contributions and publicity. The intellectual community has similarly identified itself with the research activities of the project. While financial assistance is important, there is tremendous scope for continuing intellectual cooperation in relation to archaeological excavation and conservation, historical research and information.

As Dr Ananda W.P. Guruge says in his introductory chapter, 'The UNESCO-WFP-Sri Lanka Cultural Triangle Project is therefore an invitation to the world to share not only in enjoying but also in safeguarding a common heritage hand in hand with a nation that is proud to be its custodian'.

While thanking Mr Federico Mayor, Director-General of UNESCO, for his keen interest in the Cultural Triangle Project of Sri Lanka, I have great pleasure in joining him in appealing to the international community to accomplish the objectives of the project within the envisaged time-frame.

I also wish to express my thanks to Mr Henri Lopes, Assistant Director-General for Culture at UNESCO, Mr Matthias Dermitzel, UNESCO Programme Specialist and Mr Barry Lane, UNESCO Consultant, as well as to Desamanya Dr Ananda W.P. Guruge, Chairman of the Editorial Board and Vidyajyoti Dr Roland Silva, Director-General of the Central Cultural Fund, for their efforts in bringing out this volume, not only to give the widest publicity to the work achieved, but also to seek financial and intellectual co-operation for the work that has yet to be accomplished.

D. B. Wijetunga

PREFACE

by the Hon. Ranil Wickremesinghe, Prime Minister of Sri Lanka and Chairman of the Central Cultural Fund

It is still an unquestioned fact that man is the most evolved creature in the known universe. Thus, the achievements of this being represent the highest records of any known creative genius. Considering Planet Earth as the homeland of this creature called man, there have been certain nodal points in his actions throughout history. Sri Lanka, because of its geographical situation, was such a nodal point, and many of humanity's great achievements have taken place there.

Recognizing the fact that Sri Lanka is situated at the southernmost point of mainland Asia, the earliest travellers by sea found an indispensable port of call on the shores of this country. Not only was it rich in vegetation and other natural resources, it was also a haven where sailing vessels were obliged to seek shelter while awaiting the trade winds for the onward journey. With the expansion of maritime commerce, Sri Lanka became one of the principal centres of exchange and commerce for the seafaring peoples of the ancient world, between the Mediterranean trade of the Roman Empire and the wealth of Imperial China, where goods from one region were bartered against the products of the other and from which sailors, borne by the trade winds, were home to their families. The harbour known as the Great Emporium, mentioned only once by the Greek geographer Cosmos Indicopleustes in a text dating from the sixth century A.D., was none other than Mantota in Sri Lanka.

Economically, the prosperity of ancient Sri Lanka may be attributed to the immense wealth accumulated through trade and commerce. This was then invested by the monarchs of old in their beliefs and in the religious foundations of the country. The stupas of Anuradhapura, capital of Sri Lanka for 1,300 years, which are some of the greatest achievements of the ancient world, are the tangible fruits of that prosperity. We do know that, in the fourth century A.D., with the collapse of the Roman Empire, the three tallest pyramids of Gizeh in Egypt, standing 483, 471 and 303 feet high respectively and built of stone, were the tallest group of monuments in the world. Next came the brick stupas of Anuradhapura, namely, Jetavana, Abhayagiri and Ruvanvaliseya at 404, 370 and 300 feet respectively. These monuments today still match the grandeur of their original stature as a symbol of the religious aspirations and the scientific, engineering and economic achievements of the people of our island civilization. If this is the case today, how much more so would it have been before the end of the ancient world?

The plan of Anuradhapura, capital of Sri Lanka for 1,300 years, was laid out by the father of town planning in Sri Lanka, King Pandukabhaya, in the fourth century B.C. It is this city, and the subsequent capitals of Sigiriya, Polonnaruva and Kandy, together with the colonial port of Galle, that have been identified as World Heritage Sites by UNESCO, and it is from among them that UNESCO adopted the Cultural Triangle as its nineteenth campaign, which has since proved to be one of its most successful attempts to safeguard the heritage of mankind.

We take this opportunity, in this publication covering the work of the UNESCO-Sri Lanka Project for safeguarding the principal monuments and sites of the Cultural Triangle, to thank the Member States of UNESCO for their generosity and committed support to save these Sri Lanka monuments, which are also the property of mankind, the most evolved creature of the Universe.

We also wish to thank the Director-General of UNESCO and his staff for their vision and foresight in launching such a memorable and heroic project. I am personally grateful to the dreams of my predecessors, the late President Ranasinghe Premadasa and His Excellency D.B. Wijetunga, who pioneered the work of the Cultural Triangle Project in this country. The Government of Sri Lanka, conscious of the importance of this undertaking, has provided for the highest in the land to guide this noble task of caring for these World Heritage sites. Finally, I wish to place on record on behalf of the people of Sri Lanka the nation's debt of gratitude to the many officials of the Central Cultural Fund who have given such dedicated service to a cause of such immeasurable significance.

Ranil Wickremesinghe

PREFACE

by Mr Federico Mayor, Director-General of UNESCO

Sri Lanka is the cradle of one of the great civilizations of Asia and the world. From the third century B.C., successive Buddhist kingdoms flourished within a triangular area bounded in the north by the ancient capital and sacred city of Anuradhapura, in the east by the medieval capital Polonnaruva. and in the south by Kandy, the hilltop capital of the last Sinhala king.

What is now called the Cultural Triangle was the centre from which the influence of Theravada Buddhism and Sinhala artistic genius spread far and wide. The astonishing concentration of monuments and sites, including monastic settlements, royal palaces, gardens and vast irrigation works, as well as rock paintings and sculpture, testifies to the artistic and technological achievements of those ancient kingdoms.

Launched in 1980, the international campaign to safeguard the principal monuments and sites of the Cultural Triangle is one of the largest cultural heritage projects carried out to date by UNESCO. No undertaking on such a scale has been seen in Sri Lanka itself since the time of King Parakramabahu I in the twelfth century. The excellent work already carried out has been made possible largely through the generous response of donors and is a measure of the importance attached to this campaign by the international community.

The present publication sets out to describe for the first time in a single volume the results of two decades of excavation and research by a dedicated national team to rescue lost temples and palaces from the jungle of Sri Lanka's Cultural Triangle. In particular, it provides an account – in the form of descriptions by the archaeologists and conservators concerned – of our present state of knowledge of the six major sites adopted by UNESCO for the international safeguarding campaign. This is completed by an introduction by H.E. Ananda Guruge, formerly Ambassador to UNESCO and now the Sri Lankan Ambassador in Washington, on the historical setting of the Cultural Triangle, by a postscript by Dr Roland Silva, Director-General of the Sri Lankan Central Cultural Fund and President of the International Council on Monuments and Sites, on the efforts of the Sri Lankan authorities to mobilize international support for the campaign, and by a glossary of Pali, Sinhala and Sanskrit terms.

UNESCO is pleased to have been able to lend its support to the publication of this work, which should give pleasure and instruction to the general reader as well as serving as a useful reference work for future researchers.

Federico Mayor

Contents

Introduction

From Tamraparni to Taprobane and from Ceylon to Sri Lanka

Ananda W. P. Guruge

Sri Lanka, the Resplendent Island as its current name signifies, is a land with a long, rich and colourful history.

Over a period of at least twenty-five centuries, it has been known by a variety of names, each with a geographical, ethnic or cultural significance.

Tambapanni

Sri Lanka's identity as a nation finds clear and irrefutable proof in the epigraphic records of India of the third century before Christ. Twice in his inscriptions, the Mauryan Emperor Asoka the Righteous refers to it as *Tambapanni (Tamraparni)* and marks it as the southernmost country to which he had extended his benevolent services for the benefit of man and beast (Rock Edict II) and sent messengers of peace and virtue in the course of the campaign of Conquest by Righteousness, or *Dharmavijaya* (Rock Edict XIII). The Sri Lankan historical tradition dates the founding of the nation to at least two centuries prior to these inscriptions. It further explains Tamraparni, meaning copper-coloured palms, as the name given by the founding settlers on account of the colour of the soil. In fact it was the name they gave to the township which they established at the point of landing. The region has conserved this name until today in its Sinhala form *Tammanna.*

This claim for the antiquity of both the name and the nation finds support from independent Greek sources which evince a remarkable familiarity with this island-nation in its formative years. That in itself is not surprising because the historical epic, the *Mahavamsa*, while describing the layout of the ancient capital Anuradhapura in the fourth century before Christ, speaks of its western suburb as a Greek settlement.

Taprobane

Onesicritus of Astipalacia who accompanied Alexander the Great on his eastern campaign (326 to 323 B.C.) left the earliest known record of the island, referring to it as *Taprobane*, clearly a Greek rendering of *Tamraparni.* According to Strabo, who quotes him, Onesicritus knew the size of the island, the duration of the sea voyage to it and the quality of the ships which the islanders used in their regular commercial traffic with the Indus region of the Indian subcontinent. He is also said to have recorded that the islanders had originated from this same region. Pliny the Elder also cites him as assessing its elephants as more warlike than those of India. Other

Greek works such as those of Megasthenes, Ambassador of Seleukas Nikator to the court of Candragupta Maurya (321-297 B.C.), give information on the nature, location, size, products and settlements of Taprobane.

The Romans, too, knew Sri Lanka as Taprobane and its people as *Salike* or *Salai* (Sinhala), and the earliest reference to it is by Pliny the Elder in connection with a freeman named Annius Plocamus. His accidental arrival on the island resulted in the dispatch of four ambassadors by the Sri Lankan King to the Roman court in the early years of the Christian era. This mission is echoed in the Sri Lankan tradition which records that Bhatika Abhaya (19 B.C.-A.D.9), in whose reign the envoys could have been sent, actually imported Roman coral with which to decorate the Great Thupa of Anuradhapura.

Pliny goes into details of what he had learnt of the island, its king, its produce and commercial relations, from Rachia, the head of the mission. The Latin author paints such a glowing picture of the democratic, political, administrative and judicial system of Taprobane as to suggest that he could even have idealized Sri Lanka in order to contrast it with what he wanted to criticize of the evils of contemporary Rome. However, much of Rachia's information could have been authentic, as the reign of Bhatika Abhaya and those of his immediate predecessor and successor constituted half a century of peace and prosperity. This is testified to not only by the Chronicles but also by a spate of contemporary inscriptions.

That the growing Graeco-Roman contacts with Sri Lanka resulted in an enhanced knowledge of the island, its topography, economy and culture, finds testimony in the writings and cartography of Ptolemy or Claudius Ptolomeus, the Greek geographer of Alexandria of the second century A.D. The size of Taprobane, of course, had been grossly exaggerated in relation to neighbouring India, but the topographical features, the wealth of place names, and the remarkable accuracy in the location of many of them establish the depth and sophistication of Graeco-Roman knowledge of Sri Lanka.

By the sixth century, when Cosmas Indicopleustes wrote his account of Taprobane, the country had developed its trade relations not only with the Graeco-Roman world but also with China and the Far East, and become a veritable emporium which he described as the 'mediatrix' of commerce between East and West. Concerning its role in the trade between the 'Homeric countries' and China, he says, 'Receiving in return the trafic of these markets and transmitting to the inner ports, the island exports to each of these at the same time her own products.' While he gives no information on such products, current research suggests that the major exports of Sri Lanka at that time may have been rice, elephants and iron.

Sihaladipa, Sihala, Sinhala, Sihalanam Dipa, Simhalanam Dipa

It is Cosmas who noted that the island which the pagans or Graeco-Romans called Taprobane was identified in India as *Sieladiba* (Pali *Sihaladipa*, meaning the island of the Sinhalas). The earliest epigraphic record with this name comes from a Brahmi inscription in the Tinnevely district of Tamilnadu in South India where *Sihala* occurs in its Dravidianized form Ila in reference to a family from the island. Paleographically, this inscription

is contemporary with, or slightly later than, the inscriptions of Asoka mentioned above. Two Sri Lankan inscriptions of the same period refer to the country simply as *Dipa* or Island. A further epigraphic testimony to the Indian use of derivatives from *Sihala* to refer to the island comes from the Allahabad inscription of the fourth-century Gupta Emperor Samudragupta. Here it is called *Sainhalaka*, the Land of the Sinhalas.

The Chinese, with whom trade relations had been as extensive as with the West, have participated in an even more pronounced interaction in the domain of a shared Buddhist culture. Chinese sources refer to many exchanges of cultural as well as political missions and visits of missionaries, scholars and pilgrims to and from each country. These lasted with sustained intensity until the repeated maritime expeditions of Cheng Ho which caused political havoc in Sri Lanka. With the expansion of European power in the Indian Ocean, contact with China began to dwindle.

Chinese names for the island, it is interesting to note, were derivatives of the Indian appellation *Sihaladipa*. Even if the identification of *Ssu-cheng-pu* of the History of the Han Dynasty with *Sihaladipa* as a country visited by the Chinese in the reign of Emperor P'ing (A.D. 1-6) is open to doubt, names like *Ta Shih, Ta Shi-tzu-kuo, chi-ss-tseu* and *Sang-kia-lo* are translations or transliterations of Sinhala, meaning the Lion Race.

Selendip, Serendip, Hsi-lan-ch'ih, Ceilao, Ceylan, Ceylon

In referring to the country as the Island of the Sinhala Race, both Pali and Sanskrit could use two forms: *Sihaladipa* or *Simhaladipa*, as a compound of two words, or Sihalanam dipa or Simhalanam dipa, where the first word, in the plural of the genitive case, means 'of the Sinhalas'. This usage gave a series of popular names for Sri Lanka which call for explanation.

With reference to an embassy from Sri Lanka to the court of the Byzantine Emperor Julian in A.D. 361, the name of the country is given by Ammanius

Marcellinus II as *Seren Devi*. Etymologically, this form can only be derived from *Sihalanam (Selen* or *Seren)* and *dipa (div, divi* or *dib)*.

Arab writers did not know Sri Lanka by its other names *Siyalan* or *Sihalan (Sihalam)* and *Tabrubani (Tamraparni* or *Taprobane)* but seem to have adopted the Byzantine form. Ibn Khurdab, the ninth-century Arab geographer, and Ibn Shahriyar, the tenth-century author of *Ajaib al-Hind*, actually knew that the island was called Saheelan, but preferred to adhere to the popular usage, *Sarandib*. Other writers of the same century, such as Al-Tabiri, Ishtakhri, Maqdisi and Ibn Hawqal, and later writers who provide invaluable information on a growing commercial and cultural interaction with Sri Lanka, continued to use the form *Sarandib*, pronounced Serendip or Selendip.

An epitome of all that the Arabs new and appreciated in Sri Lanka can be seen in the fascinating tales of Sinbad the Sailor in *Alf Layala wa Layla* (the Arabian Nights) about the fabulous King of Serendib. Through them, the Arabs contributed to the English language with Horace Walpole's neologism *serendipity*, meaning literally the quality of Sri Lanka and signifying the faculty of making fortunate discoveries when not in search of them.

In an isolated instance in Chinese sources, the *History of the Sung Dynasty*, describing an eleventh-century mission to the Sung court, refers to the country as *Hsi-lan-ch'ih* which appears to be a transliteration of the Arabic form *Selendib*. How prevalent this form was among the Chinese, we have no way of determining.

There is, however, no doubt that the Arab form, together with this Chinese transliteration, could have given rise to the various names that Portuguese, Dutch, French, and finally the English gave to this island: Ceilao, Ceylaan, Ceylan and Ceylon, with the pseudo-Latin form *Zeylanica*. Originating from the Pali or Sanskrit expression for the Island of the Sinhalas, all these names, including the Dravidian form *Ila* or *Ilam*, have an ethnic connotation which underscores the dominant community whose ancient ancestors had apparently adopted the totemic symbol of a lion.

Lanka and Sri Lanka

According to the Sri Lankan historical tradition, Lanka was already the name of the island before the Sinhalas under Vijaya came there. The antiquity of this name, though not epigraphically established, unlike *Tamraparni* and *Sihala*, is borne out by the great epics of India, particularly the Ramayana, whose central theme is the abduction of an Indian princess by Ravana, the Raksasa king of Sri Lanka. It is simply as *Lanka* or *Lankadipa* that the country is referred to in the Pali Chronicles and Commentaries and early Sinhala inscriptions. The corresponding Tamil form was Ilangai. The honorific *Siri* in Sinhala and Pali, and *Sri* in Sanskrit, as far as can be verified today, came to be prefixed about a millennium ago.

What was done in 1972 with the adoption of a Republican Constitution was to eliminate the difference between the national and international nomenclature, which, being a purely geographical term, meaning a Resplendent Island, is more in keeping with the rich and varied pluri-cultural character of the Nation.

Many are the other names and epithets used by those who wished to highlight the island's natural and cultural heritage. It was *Ratnadipa* to the lovers of its lustrous precious gems and *hammadipa* to those who valued its role as the home of Buddhism. In relation to India it was called *Parasamudra* in Sanskrit or *Palaesimoundu* in Greek, meaning -beyond the sea. Christian and Muslim legends equated it with the Garden of Eden to which Adam and Eve were exiled from Paradise and named its most impressive (though not its highest) mountain -Adam's Peak, and the line of islands and sandbanks between the island and India -Adam's Bridge. More widely used today are such epithets as -Tropical Paradise and -Pearl of the Indian Ocean, reflecting its bewitching scenic beauty and other natural endowments which compelled even a nineteenth-century evangelist, impatient with the island's indigenous religions, to begin his poem with 'Where every prospect pleases....

An extraordinary sense of history

The long and impressive array of names emanating from civilizations long lost merely underscores the antiquity of the country and the place it had occupied in relation to each of them. We would have learned a lot about it from all these sources. But what makes Sri Lanka unique is that it has maintained an unbroken written record of its history with a remarkably dependable chronology which enables us to understand and appreciate what the world had noted about its genius and achievements. As far as at least the neighbouring nations go, Sri Lanka demonstrated an acute sense of history very early in its formation.

The island has been inhabited since time immemorial. The stone age implements date back many thousands of years. The remains of monuments and urn burial ground speak of cultures long past and forgotten. The legends speak of a mythical king with supernatural powers and astonishing learning, whose escapades brought reprisals from a mighty monarch of India. Of the early Brahminical saints who wandered forth and established hermitages in peninsular India, two at least, Agastya and Pulasti, are associated with the island. The national chronicles refer to Yakkhas and Nagas, with high levels of material culture, who were already present when the Aryans first arrived here. Excavations at the citadel of Anuradhapura have brought to light artifacts which push back the beginnings of the history of Sri Lanka by several centuries.

The island which had for several millennia been a centre of human activity was colonized by migrants from north-western India who came from overseas. This is a common basis for several legends pertaining to the first waves of settlers. The one that the national chronicles record relates to an exiled prince from Sinhapura in Lata (probably in Gujerat) whose ship was washed ashore. Aided by a princess of the Yakkha tribe whom he makes his consort, Vijaya establishes the Kingdom of Sri Lanka and with this event begins its written history. A township at the point at which they landed, and which they called Tambapanni, became its seat of government.

With a queen for himself and wives for his followers obtained from the Pandyans of southern Madura across the Palk's Straight, another Aryan-speaking community which had made an incursion to the south, Vijaya ruled for thirty-eight years. He wished his brother from Sinhapura to be his successor, but instead it was his nephew who took his place. This king, Panduvasudeva, chose his queen from among a wave of migrants from a royal family of the Indo-Gangetic basin. Vijaya's own followers and the brothers of the new queen established their principalities all over the island. Thus was established a new nation which was apparently so proud of its achievements in the new land that it sought ways and means to assert its political and cultural identity. This was further necessitated by the presence of a solid block of Dravidian cultures in the region of India closest to the island. Historiography was their chosen method of asserting and accentuating their national and cultural identity.

So complete and authentic are their records that places can still be identified and statistics appear plausible. A seventeen-year campaign by a rebel prince to gain the throne has been described in such detail as not only to make it possible for us to trace its progress, but also to understand the strategical significance of each of his moves and the locations of his military operations. The monks who later compiled the national chronicles could not have been so comprehensive unless the original records were themselves purposely prepared as works of history. A tradition of secular court history thus became part of the Sri Lankan cultural heritage.

Anuradhapura was founded by this rebel prince who became king under the name of Pandukabhaya. The first ruler to be actually born on the island, he not only brought together the original settlers of the island to collaborate with the Sinhalas, but also demarcated village boundaries for the whole country. The establishment of Anuradhapura as a well-planned city was his major achievement. So appropriate was its location both geographically and strategically that it served the nation as a flourishing centre of economic and cultural activity for at least twelve centuries.

It was at the time of his grandson, King Devanampiya, that the close and persisting interaction with Aryan-speaking kingdoms of Northern India brought Sri Lanka into direct contact with the Mauryan Empire. Tissa as a prince is said to have been an 'unseen friend' - a pen-pal - of Emperor Asoka, and the first task he is recorded as having performed on assumption of kingship was to send an embassy with gifts to the Mauryan court. Asoka had him crowned a second time, this time according to Mauryan ritual, and apparently Tissa assumed the honorific *Devanampiya* either in emulation or as an indication of some political liaison. Whatever may be the case, it was from this friendship with Asoka that the momentous event of the introduction of Buddhism to Sri Lanka derived in the first year of Devanampiya Tissa's reign and the eighteenth year of Asoka's, 236 years after the death of the Buddha.

As far as historiography is concerned, the arrival of Buddhism, with its unique institution of the self-renewing intellectual community of monks and nuns, together called the *Samgha*, gave an unprecedented stimulus. If the court historians recorded events to assert and maintain national cultural identity, Buddhism found in historical recording two major uses. Firstly, as Buddhism spread in and outside its region of origin,it became necessary to establish the authenticity of its doctrine by tracing the history of the linear descent of the tradition. Secondly, Buddhism subsisted on public charity, and grateful recording of services rendered to it was a *sine qua non* for drawing in more donors. If, with the introduction of Buddhism, Sri Lanka entered into the phase which scholars tend to call 'writing history for a purpose', the benefit has been remarkable.

The earliest works of conscious history in Sri Lanka were the historical introductions to the Sinhala commentaries on the Buddhist cannon. This massive literary venture is attributed to the royal missionary Thera Mahinda who, with his sister Theri Sanghamitta, both children of the Emperor Asoka, devoted their entire lives to the cause of Buddhism in the island. These introductions, called the *Sihala-Atthakatha-Mahavamsa*, were periodically updated and a history of Buddhism in Sri Lanka, which could not be totally dissociated from that of the nation, was the result.

Over the last one hundred and fifty years, archaeological research in India and Sri Lanka has confirmed the historical authenticity of these early records. Without them the identification of Emperor Asoka with the *Devanapiya* of his numerous inscriptions would have been delayed by nearly a century. Names found on the reliquaries of the stupas of Sanchi and Sonari in India would have been meaningless without the data from Sri Lankan historical tradition. In fact, the reconstruction of a considerable portion of ancient Indian history has been facilitated by these records.

The earliest known attempt in Sri Lanka to present its historical record in the form of chronicles dates back to about the fourth century. The *Dipavamsa* was undoubtedly a tentative first effort and contains all the blemishes of linguistic solicisms, bad organization, contradictions and repetitions. But its value as an attempt to present a concise history of nearly eight hundred years in Pali verse is remarkable. Remedying the defects of this first Chronicle, Thera Mahanama of the sixth century produced the *Mahavamsa* covering the same period in more elegant Pali verse with far greater success from both literary and historical standpoints. It has since become the national epic which has been prolonged from time to time in identical literary form. It has been brought up to 1956, and has rightly been called Sri Lanka's non-stop epic.

The most significant achievement of the *Mahavamsa* is that it began as and continued to be an amalgam of both the court tradition of history and monastic history. In a sense of objectivity rarely found in sectarian writing, it is fair in its assessment of foreign invaders. Even the South Indian ruler whose deposition by the national hero is the central theme of the Mahavamsa is praised for his impartial justice during his reign. So are two earlier invaders described as having ruled the island righteously.

Both these Chronicles serve the modern researcher as his most indispensable tool. To the archaeologist, they are essential field manuals in locating and identifying the monuments. To the epigraphist, they and they alone have enabled him to identify the writers of inscriptions, determine the accuracy of the reading and interpret the historical evidence they present. The chronological framework which they present continues to be the cornerstone of Sri Lankan history, in spite of the fact that some lacunae remain to be filled concerning the earlier period.

Later chronicles and works of history

Apart from commentaries and glossaries written to these chronicles, the historiographers of Sri Lanka down the ages produced an enormous number of specialized works in which the history of sacred objects and places was recounted. These works were in both Sinhala and Pali and constitute a class of literature called *Vamsakatha*. Substantial chapters in the narrative Buddhist literature in Sinhala, the extant works of which date back to the thirteenth century but are still read by the general public, are devoted to recounting continuous history or historical episodes. The Sinhala people seem to have had a compulsive interest in history.

Even at times of nation-wide political havoc as in the days of the Portuguese and Dutch wars with independent Sinhala kingdoms, a series of war ballads, called *Hatan Kavya*, was composed which, though poor in literary quality, is invaluable as a source of contemporary history. Equally impressive are manuals such as *Rajavaliya* and *Rajaratnakaraya*, written to cater to popular demand for simple works on history. Temple libraries are replete with innumerable historical documents in the form of *vittipot* (books of information) and *kadayapot* (books on boundaries), awaiting publication and study. The catalogue of the collection in the British Museum alone would show a nation which began to keep historical records at the earliest stages of its formation and has continued to do so up to modern times.

Historical research today

Edward Upham, in a somewhat imperfect way, drew the attention of the West to Sri Lankan historical tradition in 1833. But with the publication of the *Mahavamsa* by George Turner in 1837, the *Dipavamsa* by Herman Oldenberg in 1879, and the prolongations of the *Mahavamsa* by L.C. Wijesinha in 1899, the study of Sri Lankan history has been pursued in many a centre of learning in the world. Over a hundred years ago the Archaeological Survey of Ceylon began to address itself to the excavation and conservation of and research into several hundred monuments in all parts of the island. Its reports are among the most comprehensive ever made. A few thousand inscriptions have also been found, deciphered and published. Mural paintings dating from the fifth century at hundreds of sites have been catalogued and documented. Yet much awaits the attention of the serious scholar, and *Serendipity* could still be his motivation and reward.

Landmarks in history

Tradition places the arrival of the Aryans under Vijaya in the same year as the death of the Buddha, but scholars wish to keep an open mind with regard to the exact date as some of the reigns of the ancient kings appear to have been distorted to effect such a coincidence. Vijaya reigned for thirty-eight years and is reported to have stated that during this period, 'This kingdom was founded with difficulty'. In all likelihood he had to deal with resistance from the original settlers. Throughout the reign of his successor, Panduvasudeva, a nephew invited from the old country, much of the resistance appears to have continued. Though not recorded in the chronicles, somewhat mythicized incidents of his reign continue to be recalled in ritual chants connected with exorcism ceremonies.

A clandestine love affair between his daughter and the nephew of his queen produced the first 'all Sri Lankan' contender to the throne. Escaping a series of attempts made by his maternal uncles to kill him while still a child, this Pandukabhaya leads a successful rebellion against them. As mentioned earlier, he assumed the throne after a seventeen-year campaign. Apart from his achievements in town and country planning and the reconciliation with earlier settlers, he also initiated the tradition of constructing reservoirs and possibly canals for irrigation, an enterprise for which the fame that Sri Lanka has attracted for its technological ingenuity displayed in gigantic projects is more than justified.

Relations with the Mauryan Empire had commenced during the reign of his son Mutasiva. It was at the very beginning of the reign of his son Tissa or Devanampiya Tissa that Buddhism was introduced to Sri Lanka along with the technological and cultural achievements of the Mauryan civilization. This was undoubtedly the most important event in the nation's history.

The island had been the meeting ground of several sects and religious persuasions which developed in the Indo-Gangetic basins of Northern India. Brahmans had established Vedic schools and served as chaplains to kings. Jains and Ajivakas had sites allotted to them in fourth-century Anuradhapura. Yet Buddhism, right from its advent, became the dominant religion primarily because the king, the royal family and the courtiers were the first to embrace it. The exemplary devotion of the two royal missionaries and the local *Samgha* which they created was a further reason. The continuing support which the Mauryan Emperor gave by sending the Bodhi-tree and the bodily relics of the Buddha was certainly very reassuring. The fact that the kinsmen of Asoka who came with the Bodhi-tree formed a hereditary bureaucracy and assumed reponsiblility for the administration of the island could also have helped the process.

Buddhism gave Sri Lankans a serene philosophy of life which served as an enduring source of inspiration for their creativity in art, architecture and literature. Mention was made earlier of the massive literature that was produced in the form of extensive commentaries on the Buddhist canon. Reference is made to poetical compositions on Buddhist themes. Several inscriptions in early Brahmi script were found to be in Sinhala verse.

In the reign of Devanampiya Tissa, the establishment of two main monasteries at Anuradhapura (Mahavihara) and Mihintale (Cetiyapabbata) and the construction of Thuparama as the first Stupa were followed by a network of Buddhist shrines throughout the country at regular intervals of seven or eight miles. Each of them was a veritable educational institution where the *Samgha* exerted its remarkable role as an agent of civilization. The promotion of Buddhism came to be recognized consciously or otherwise as the national mission. Thousands of early Brahmi inscriptions recording donations to Buddhist shrines by people of all races, classes and occupations testify to the extent of popular patronage which Buddhism received.

The southern Kingdom of Ruhunu

A court intrigue compelled Mahanaga, the sub-king of Devanampiya Tissa, to seek his fortunes in southern Sri Lanka where he first served some local rulers as commander of their Javanese (Javaka) forces. In due course, he carved out for himself a principality with Magama (the present-day Tissamaharama) as its capital. Within decades, Anuradhapura was overrun by Elara from Cola in South India and the area which constitutes roughly today's northern, north-central and north-western provinces was ruled by him for forty-four years. The kings of Magama and Kelaniya remained independent and carried on the tradition of promoting Buddhism. To them goes the credit for founding the great monasteries of Situlpavva and Tissamaharama in the south, Seruvila in the north-east and a considerable number of local shrines. They maintained a policy of co-existence with Elara, until Dutthagamani Abhaya, the son of the king of Magama by the daughter of the king of Kelaniya, found it necessary to reunify the country.

Declaring his effort to be motivated by a committment to promote Buddhism, Dutthagamani Abhaya led a successful campaign against Elara, whom he slew in single combat. His reign of twenty-four years (161-137 B.C.) saw the heyday of Buddhism. He built the Mirisavatiya Stupa and established a monastery around it. For the Mahavihara, he constructed the *Lovamahapaya* (Brazen Palace), the ten-storeyed, thousand-roomed dwelling place for monks. The pinnacle of his achievements as a great builder was the Ruvanvalisaya, the oldest of the three giant brick stupas of Anuradhapura. Buddhist India had nothing of the magnitude of either this stupa or the Brazen Palace. Elsewhere, only the two great pyramids of Egypt surpassed them in height. As far as brick structures are concerned, however, they had no parallel anywhere.

A lasting contribution to Buddhism

Just four decades later, chaotic conditions caused by a Brahmin in revolt, an invasion from South India, the usurpation of the throne by five Tamil rulers in succession and a twelve-year drought tested the ingenuity of the Buddhist *Samgha*.

Depleting ranks and the hazards of sickness and death convinced them that the practice of preserving the Buddhist Canon and its commentaries through oral transmission had to be rethought. Thus, when Valagamba (89-77 B.C.) regained the throne, the monks assembled at Aluvihara near Matale and committed all the texts to writing. The far-reaching impact of this exercise could best be gauged by the fact that only the Theravada Pali canon of Sri Lanka has been preserved in its pristine form. The Sinhala Commentaries lasted for several centuries, even after they were translated into Pali, the *lingua franca* of the Buddhist world, in the fifth century, and are found quoted in Sinhala works of the tenth and twelfth centuries.

Another major event in the reign of Valagambahu was the establishment of the Abhayagiri monastery on the site of a Jaina temple. Up to the reign of Valagambahu, the Buddhist monastic system was unitary in character and all institutions were affiliated to the Mahavihara, which jealously guarded its rights and privileges as the custodian of orthodoxy. Abhayagiri unintentionally became the seat of dissident monks and developed into a parallel institution. In due course, it adopted a more open policy to new developments in Buddhism. The rivalry between the conservative Mahavihara and the progressive Abhayagiri provided the

stimulus for the spiritual and intellectual life of the nation for several centuries. Royal patronage was usually extended to both, although major conflicts occurred when that impartiality was not observed.

The struggle for power between Valagambahu's son who was denied the throne and his nephew and adopted son who became king resulted in a period of political upheaval. It was then that Anula, the wife of the former, successively disposed of four husbands, each of whom she placed on the throne. Among them were an Indian architect, a Tamil Brahmin chaplain, and a wood-carrier. Finally, she herself ascended to the throne for only four months, before being ousted by Kutakannatissa (44-22 B.C.), an erstwhile crown prince who had become a Buddhist monk in order to escape her wrath. The half-century that followed was an era of peace which saw a number of excessively pious kings whose preoccupations were more with popular Buddhist ceremonies than with matters of State. The country had been well-administered, however, and foreign trade flourished. It was one of these kings who sent the embassy to the Roman court.

Rise of the Lambakannas

The Vijaya-Pandukabhaya dynasty which had ruled Sri Lanka hitherto was beginning to degenerate. It came to a point where there was no one who could claim the right to the throne through descent from a male member of the royal family. Once again a queen ascended the throne and she too lasted only four months. The reign of the usurper did not last long either because the hereditary bureaucracy, composed of the Lambakanna clan, had by then gained enough control over the nation to found its own dynasty. The first two attempts were somewhat tentative. Ilanaga (A.D. 35-44) had to obtain support from South India when he was thrown out by the Lambakannas. This support had to be sealed by a matrimonial alliance, and his son ascended the throne with a Tamil queen.

His brother, Yasalalaka Tissa (A.D. 52-59), a fun-loving king, was the victim of one of his own practical jokes. The door-keeper with whom he exchanged places to tease the ministers took the opportunity to punish with death the door-keeper for his impudence. Thus the first Lambakanna came to power and ruled for six years. He was overthrown by another Lambakanna, Vasabha (A.D. 65-109) who ruled the country for forty-four years and whose record of public service evinces the management style and capacity of the Lambakannas. Once in the seat of power, this clan, with its long administrative traditions and experience, made the king more visible as not merely the protector of the Faith, but above all the focus of national development in all aspects. Vasabha's well-documented record of major irrigation projects and services to Buddhism is indeed very impressive. He left many inscriptions which corroborate and confirm the information in the Chronicles. It was during this period that the hydraulic engineering works of Sri Lanka received a significant impetus, apparently because rice-growing for export had become a principal element of the economy.

With Vasabha began more than a century (A.D. 67-188) of peace and prosperity, free from invasion and internal strife. Besides the information in the Chronicles, a fair number of inscriptions describe in detail the activities of his four successors.

Ruvanvalisaya, Anuradhapura.
Originally constructed by king Dutugemunu in the 2nd century B.C. Restored in the early 20th century.

Vasabha's grandson, Gajabahu I, who is credited with victory in a raid against the Colas, befriended the Cera (Kerala) king Senguttuvan and was present when he consecrated a shrine for the Goddess Pattini. Not only did he introduce the Pattini cult to Sri Lanka, but he also supported the Abhayagiri. The original stupa of this monastery built by Valagamba was enlarged to be larger than the Ruvanvalisaya of Dutthagamani. But, apparently to maintain the policiy of impartiality, he fitted a mantle to the Mirisavatiya stupa of the Mahavihara. But a measure of special attention to the Abhayagiri is recorded in the reign of one of his successors when facilities for it were built by encroaching on the premises traditionally held by the Mahavihara.

Dynastic changes within the Lambakanna clan

A dynastic change within the Lambakanna clan itself, caused most probably by a severe famine when grain had to be rationed, brought Sirinaga I (195-214) to the throne. His first decree was to abolish a grain tax. He appears to have favoured the Mahavihara in that he rebuilt the Brazen Palace, added a stone parasol to the Ruvanvalisaya and restored the stairway of the Bodhi-tree.

His son Voharikatissa or Tissa the Legal-minded (A.D. 209-31) reformed the judicial system to eliminate repression and carried out an impartial religious policy. The earliest recorded instance of the introduction of the Mahayana form of Buddhism was in his reign. He had the doctrines examined by a Minister named Kapila and had them refuted. His end, however, was sad because his unfaithful wife and disloyal brother engineered a revolution against him.

Hardly a decade passed without a strange event in the history of Sri Lanka happening. Three adventurers who had no connection with the capital and no claim to the throne succeeded in overthrowing Vijayakumara in the first year of his reign and assumed kingship in succession.

The first of them was poisoned to death by people who were harassed by royal visits to their village; the king went there too often with his large entourage because he was fond of a particular fruit. The second, Sirisamgabodi (247-49), was a veritable saint who decided to take his own life in order to prevent innocent people from being killed in his name. He continues to be venerated as the national paragon of piety and virtue.

The last of them, Gothabhaya (253-66), established a dynasty which lasted several centuries and produced some of the most able monarchs of Sri Lanka. He was partial to the Mahavihara and remodelled its buildings, besides renovating dilapidated monastic residences throughout the island.

Challenge to the Mahavihara

The Mahayana form of Buddhism was introduced again to Sri Lanka and this time it actually received the support of the Abhayagiri monastery. Gothabhaya was determined to suppress the heretics. Not only did he rebuke sixty monks who upheld Mahayana doctrines but had them branded and exiled to South India. This incident was the cause of a most serious conflict between the Mahavihara and the Abhayagiri in the reign of his second son a decade later.

His elder son, Jetthatissa, is remembered particularly for the dastardly massacre of his enemies at the time of his father's funeral, although he, too, was a patron of the Mahavihara. He completed the seven-storeyed Brazen Palace which his father had begun.

A Cola monk, a disciple of one the Abhayagiri monks, branded and exiled to South India by Gothabhaya, had come to Anuradhapura with the specific purpose of avenging the humiliation of his teacher, Sanghamitta. This monk won the favour of Gothabhaya and became tutor to his two sons. Yet it was the younger prince who was more amenable to him.

Thus when Mahasena (277-303) became king, he began his campaign against the Mahavihara, the seat of orthodoxy. A royal decree was obtained to forbid charity to it on pain of heavy fines. Without lay support, the monastery could not last and it was closed for nine years. Using the law that unoccupied property belonged to the crown, buildings of the Mahavihara were torn down and the material used to erect new buildings for the Abhayagiri. The Chronicle says that this monastery became rich with buildings and very attractive.

The destruction of the venerable monastery reached such a point that one of the king's ministers, who was also his closest friend, took up arms. On the eve of the battle, however, their friendship prevailed over their differences. The minister found in his dinner hamper a curry which the king enjoyed most. So he walked over to the royal camp, shared the dinner with the king, talked things over and convinced the king. Bereft of Mahasena's support, Sanghamitta fell victim to the people's wrath. But the tranquillity of the Mahavihara was short-lived. Another monk, who had become the king's favourite, persuaded him to carve out a part of the premises of the Mahavihara and build a monastery for him.

This monastery, the Jetavana, with a stupa larger and taller than the two gigantic stupas of Dutthagamani and Valagamabahu/Gajabahu, became the third monastic system of the island, rivalling both the Mahavihara and the Abhayagiri for separate recognition.

As this monastic complex itself shows, Mahasena was an unrivalled builder. He established at least nine monasteries and two nunneries. But his greatest achievements were in the provision of water resources. He built as many as sixteen giant reservoirs and diverted the water of the Mahavaliganga with a canal. The technological perfection of his system of providing water resources win the admiration of modern enginners who with minimum renovation of his dams and spills have managed to incorporate many of them in the development of the North-Central Province. Mahasena's own contemporaries expressed their gratitude by deifying him and he is still worshipped in a temple near his largest construction, the Minneriya Tank.

Beginning of the Lesser Dynasty

Both the Chronicles, the Dipavamsa and the Mahavamsa, end with the reign of Mahasena. The kings that followed are said to belong to the 'Lesser Dynasty . The reason for this divison is not easy to unravel. But it seems to have had some special significance for the ancient historiographers.

The reign of Mahasena's son and successor, Kirti Siri Mevan (303-331) was marked by two significant contacts with India. Recorded in a Chinese narrative and confirmed by an inscription at Buddha Gaya itself is his mission to the Gupta Emperor, Samudragupta, to provide accommodation at this holy site for Sri Lankan pilgrims. It is no doubt due to the reputation of Sri Lanka as a haven for Buddhism that the Tooth Relic of the Buddha was brought from Kalinga when its security there was in peril. One of his decrees was drafted to the effect that the Tooth Relic should be taken to the Abhayagiri monastery each year.

Kit Siri Mevan himself and his immediate successors were cultured men of learning and artistic attainments. His sense of history is evinced by the steps taken to raise the awareness of the historic role of Thera Mahinda who introduced Buddhism to the island. His brother who succeeded him was a sculptor who specialized in ivory carving and set up institutions to train people. The next in line, Buddhadasa (341-370), was a remarkable physician and is accredited with the Sanskrit work on medicine, *Sararthasangraha*. It was during his reign that the Suttas of the Buddhist Canon were first translated from Pali into Sinhala.

Mahanama (412-434) saw a period of important activities in both the Mahavihara and the Abhayagiri. It was at this time that Thera Buddhaghosa sought permission from the Mahavihara to translate the Sinhala Commentaries on the Buddhist Canon into Pali. He had to write the *Visuddhimagga* to prove his competence before such permission was given. The Abhayagiri for two years hosted the Chinese pilgrim, Fa-hsien, who had come to study Theravada Buddhism and copy sacred writings. Mahanama also sent embassies to both China and Rome.

The twenty-five year period which followed the reign of Mahanama was chaotic and led to one when as many as six South Indian invaders took advantage of the confusion. Order was restored by Dhatusena (459-477) who, too, demonstrated scholarly interests. He organized a rehearsal of the Buddhist Canon by the monks, an exercise similar to the Third Council attributed to Asoka. He had the history of the island explained and it is thought that the *Mahavamsa* was written by Thera Mahanama during his reign. But Dhatusena fell victim to a palace conspiracy and was buried alive by his second son Kasyapa. The heir apparent to the throne, Mugalan, fled to South India to seek support.

A golden age of art, architecture and literature

Denounced by the *Samgha* as a parricide and fearing reprisals by his brother, Kasyapa (477-495) established his capital at Sigiriya where he built his fortress on top of the rock and planted gardens at the gates of the city. He is reputed to have planted mango groves at intervals of seven or eight miles throughout the island. Apparently influenced by the cultural revival of India under the Guptas, as most of his predecessors probably were, his contribution to art and architecture, specially landscape architecture, stands as a permanent monument to a monarch who fancied himself a god and created an environment of beauty and grace all around him. After eighteen years, Moggallana returned with mercenaries from India. In the ensuing battle Kasyapa's elephant turned to avoid a swamp and the army fled under the impression that the king was retreating. Left alone, he killed himself before the enemy could reach him.

Moggallana bestowed the monasteries near Sigiriya to the monks of the *Dhammaruci* (Abhayagiri) and *Sagaliya* (Jetavana) and the Sigiriya itself to Mahanama, the author of the *Mahavamsa*. The fact that the three monastic complexes, which have each developed into a sect or school, were equally recognized and flourished together as part of a highly evolved *Mahayana* cult, with invaluable works of art found particularly along the east coast from Tiriray to Weligama and its hinterland, also suggests active intercourse with *Mahayana* Buddhists in the Near and Far East.

Anuradhapura regained its position as capital. The son and successor of Kumaradasa (512-520) is reputed to have written the Sanskrit ornate poem, the *Janakiharana*, on the theme of the abduction of Sita by Ravana. After a struggle for succession in which one king ruled nine months, another only twenty-five days and a third barely a year, a measure of stability returned in the reigns of Silakala (522-535) and Moggallana II (535-555). The former supported the *Mahayana* form of Buddhism while the other was a poet.

The long reign of Aggabodhi I (575-608) and that of his successor Aggabodhi II (608-618) are remarkable for achievements in every field. Literature flourished and as many as twelve famous poets are mentioned. The graffiti on the Sigiriya Mirror Wall would corroborate the popularity of Sinhala verse. Thera Jotipala, who vanquished the Mahayanists, attained such fame that a king of Kalinga, appalled by the horrors of war, came to Sri Lanka and became a monk in his monastery. Both kings carried on an extensive programme for the development of water resources. But with their reigns a glorious period of peace and prosperity - and especially of art, architecture and literature - came to an end.

Rise of Tamil influence in Court

Too frequently had the contenders to the throne in the preceding period fled to South India and sought the aid of mercenaries. A growing presence of Tamils near the vortex of power was inevitable. In the period following Agbo II, they wielded decisive influence as to the occupants of the throne.

It was during this period of seven decades of war and rebellion that the Chinese pilgrim, Hiuen Tsang, cooled his heels in South India awaiting an opportunity to pursue his search for Buddhist texts and teachings in Sri Lanka. So prolonged was the struggle that he had to be satisfied with data he could collect from visitors.

There was a slight respite in the reign of Aggabodhi IV (667-683). In later years, however, he had to abandon Anuradhapura and take to Polonnaruva. At his death the actual government of the country passed into the hands of his Tamil general, Potthakuttha. The long reigns of Manavamma (684-718) and Aggabodhi Salamevan (733-772) were not totally free of internal dissension, and the latter's successor was also forced to leave Anuradhapura and rule temporarily from Polonnaruva. For some time both alternated as seats of government as the security situation demanded. But finally, in the reign of Sena I (833-853), a Pandyan invasion sacked Anuradhapura and plundered its treasures.

The shift of the capital to Polonnaruva was inevitable, even though Sena I's successor Sena II (853-887) avenged the sacking of Anuradhapura by supporting a disgruntled Pandyan prince, besieging and sacking Madura and recovering the lost treasures of Sri Lanka.

Involvement in South Indian politics: the Cola invasion

Three decades later, relations with the Pandyans had changed and Kasyapa V sent a sizeable army to aid the Pandya king against his Cola adversary. When on a second occasion a Pandyan king sought assistance, Duppala V (939-940) was unable to oblige due to internal dissensions. The king left behind his regalia, which led to the invasion by the Cola king, Parantaka, demanding that these be surrendered, but Udaya III drove him back.

With South India becoming more and more instrumental in the peace and security of Sri Lanka, the kings began to look for other alliances. Mahinda IV married a princess from Kalinga. His victory over a South Indian invader brought Sri Lanka a measure of fame, but it was short-lived. By the time Mahinda V came to the throne, all he could do for nearly 24 years was to feign a semblance of authority from Ruhuna while the Tamils who rebelled against him for non-payment of wages actually controlled the rest of the island.

It was this situation which emboldened the Cola Emperor Rajaraja the Great to send an army to take Mahinda V and his queen to South India as captives and to annex Sri Lanka as a province of the growing Cola Empire. For nearly seventy-five years, this domination continued. During the first twelve years a Cola viceroy administered the province with Polonnaruva, renamed Jananatha-mangalam, as the seat of government.

Cultural achievements amidst political upheavals

In spite of these upheavals, several kings of this period took steps to reform the *Samgha*, lay down rules of discipline for Brahman priests, codify laws including cast rulings, and reform the judiciary. Art and literature appear to have flourished.

If Sena I was actually the author of *Siyabaslakara*, the very need for such a sophisticated rendering of a standard work on rhetorics in Sanskrit suggests the level of refinement to which poetry had developed. Still extant is the impressive glossary which Kasyapa V wrote on the *Commentary on the Dhammapada*. Sena IV was a reputed Buddhist scholar well versed in the doctrine and expounded it to a joint assembly of the three sects or schools of Buddhism in the country.

Many of the recent findings of Buddhist sculpture, especially of Mahayana Bodhisattvas and Taras in bronze, are also datable to this period. It is recorded that Tantric Buddhism made its first appearance in the reign of Sena II.

Foreign trade had continued unabated and a Muslim traveller, Abu Zeid, records in the tenth century that Adam's Peak had become a place of regular pilgrimage for Muslims. He was impressed by the interest the Buddhists took in copying their scriptures and also noted the high level of religious tolerance that existed on the island.

From Vijayabahu I to Parakramabahu the Great

Whatever the position of the northern part of the island as a province of the Cola Empire, the region to the east and south of the Mahavaliganga maintained a degree of independence. As many as six rulers, not all of Sri Lankan origin, exercised power until Kirti, a descendant of Mahinda V, became king under the name of Vijayabahu in 1065.

Ten rulers contended for power over the next fifteen years. Among them were the queens of Parakramabahu I and Kirti Nissankamalla. In fact, Lilavati, the queen of the former, ascended the throne three times and ruled for a total of less than six years. Kalyanavati was queen for six years from 1202 to 1208. This troubled period culminated in the invasion of Magha from Kalinga, which tolled the death knell not only of Polonnaruva as a capital, but also of Sri Lanka as a unified kingdom.

The death of Vijayabahu I in 1120 was followed by a period of turmoil. The island once again regained its glory under the reign of Parakramabahu I, who restored Anuradhapura and Polonnaruva and beautified them with gardens, fortified the city of Polonnaruva and built himself a seven-storeyed palace there.

His most spectacular achievements, however, were in the field of hydrological engineering; he worked on the principle, 'Let not a single drop of rain that falls on the island flow into the ocean without first serving the people.' As the skills needed were no longer available, he instituted a programme of retraining craftsmen such as wood and ivory carvers to handle major public works. Apart from restoring many ancient tanks and reservoirs, he himself built the impressive 'Sea of Parakrama' at Polonnaruva and a hundred-mile long canal feeding several reservoirs in the region. He was also a great warrior and his military prowess gave him the confidence to send a punitive expedition against the King of Myanmar and wage a successful war in South India.

The most noteworthy contribution of Parakramabahu was in the reunification of the Samgha. His reform process reconciled the three sects or schools: Abhayagiri, Jetavana and Mahavihara. The impetus his patronage gave to Buddhism paved the way for the spread of Theravada Buddhism to South-East Asia. Monks like Capata of Myanmar came to Sri Lanka to benefit from the revival of Buddhist educational institutions. Similarly, Sri Lankan scholars went to Malaysia, Myanmar and Thailand to teach Buddhism.

Parakramabahu I was followed by his nephew Vijayabahu II, a scholar and poet whose letters in Pali, written in his own hand to King Ramanna of Myanmar, restored cordial relations with that kingdom. Within a year the throne passed into the hands of the Kalinga race. Kirti Nissankamalla (1187-96) has left a number of boastful inscriptions and it is apparent that he claimed credit for work actually done by his uncle Parakramabahu I.

Ten rulers contended for power over the next fifteen years. Among them were the queens of Parakramabahu I and Kirti Nissankamalla. In fact, Lilivati, the queen of the former, ascended the throne three times and ruled for a total of less than six years. Kalyanavati was queen for six years from 1202 to 1208. This troubled period culminated in the invasion of Magha from Kalinga, which tolled the death knell not only of Polonnaruva as a capital, but also of Sri Lanka as a unified kingdom.

Technical and cultural progress

Despite political upheavals in the initial stages, the reigns of both Vijayabahu I and Parakramabahu I are characterized by significant achievements in the technological and cultural fields. The high level of technology in the Polonnaruva period is manifest in impressive monuments, both religious and secular, the unprecedented magnitude of irrigation schemes, the planning of the city, the precision of the measuring and surgical instruments found at the hospital of Alahana Parivena and the quality of pottery, ceramics and metal artefacts.

Buddhism made giant strides and Sri Lanka became the religious metropolis of the whole of South-East Asia. A Thai monarch held up the life of a Sri Lankan monk as a model for spiritual progress. Sinhala literary works were studied, copied, preserved and imitated in those countries, and the study of Sri Lankan history seems to have had a special attraction. The *Extended Mahavamsa*, available only in manuscript in Cambodian script, was a product of that region.

The architectural innovations were as notable as the artistic creativity and made each building, park or water tank an exceptional work of art. A two-way influence is traceable in this field, notably between Sri Lanka and Thailand. Breathtaking creations in mural painting as well as sculpture in bronze, stone and stucco have survived to the present day. Tivamka Pilimage, Galvihara, Lankatilaka, Nissanka Latamandapa, the Council Chamber of Parakramabahu and the Vatadages of Medirigiriya and Polonnaruva are but a few examples of the grandeur of Polonnaruva art. Even a Sri Lankan school of Hindu iconography seems to have evolved as reflected in some of the finest bronze statues of Nataraja, Ganesa, Siva and Parvati, and Hindu saints.

Sinhala had developed into an expressive language capable of producing ornate poetry as well as prose comparable with the finest works of Sanskrit literature. *Gi* poems like *Muvadev da vata, Sasa da vata*, and particularly *Kavsilumina*, a beautiful poem in the strictest traditions of a Sanskrit *Mahakavya*, are among the finest achievements of the intense literary activity of the period. Sanskrit begins to have an increasing impact on the literary style of Sinhala prose, and Tamil appears in inscriptions both in the capital and elsewhere. The momentum in intellectual pursuits created in this period was such that it survived a long period of disruption and near-anarchy.

The fall of Polonnaruva and the drift to the south-west

To Magha (1225-36) is attributed a veritable reign of terror and destruction. Torture, extortion, pillaging of holy shrines and monuments and book-burning marked his twenty-one year reign, which the chronicles record as the darkest age in the country's history. The glory of Anuradhapura and Polonnaruva disappeared, never to return.

Leaving Magha to rule the northern part of the island, Sinhala rulers moved gradually to the south-west of the island. Vijayabahu III (1232-36) and his son Parakramabahu II ruled from Dambadeniya. It was in the reign of the latter and his successor Vijayabahu IV that Sri lanka had to deal

with two invasions by a prince named Candrabhanu from Malaysia.

The capital moved from Dambadeniya to Yapahuva and thence to Kurunegala and Gampola, but in reality the island was no longer a unified kingdom. Many autonomous states under rulers of varying status and power had divided the country amongst themselves. A series of invasions brought about a marked Tamil presence on the island, particularly in the north. According to tradition, the Pandyan general Aryacakravarti invaded Sri Lanka in 1284 and was requested by a chieftain in Jaffna to establish the Tamil kingdom in the north with Nallur as its capital.

At the same time, Sri Lanka had maintained its trade and cultural relations with both east and west. Arab traders settled down and Muslim saints, as in South-East Asia, were active in propagating their religion. The trade mission of Bhuvanekabahu I of Yapahuva to Egypt in 1283 and the travels of Ibn Batuta in the island in 1344 are indicative of the close relations with the Middle-East.

The long-standing religious and commercial relations with China turned sour when the repeated invasions of Cheng Ho culminated in 1408 in the capture of the Sinhala king, who was taken prisoner along with his family and transported to China, where they were released on condition that a new king be appointed. Accordingly, Parakramabahu VI was chosen as king, and ruled for fifty-two years from 1420 to 1467. It is recorded that Sri Lanka was required to pay tribute to the Chinese Emperor for the next fifty years.

Galpota, Stone Inscription, Polonnaruva, 12th century.
A colosal stone inscription by King Nissankamalla

Religious and cultural activity amidst political chaos

As already stated, religious and cultural activities persisted in spite of the chaotic political situation. Sri Lanka's contribution to the spread of Buddhism, especially in South-East Asia, was redoubled and marked progress made on the island itself regarding the development of Buddhist institutions. Rules of conduct for the Samgha were promulgated under royal auspices.

Scholarship reached a very high level. Verbatim translations of major Buddhist treatises marked a transition from Pali to Sinhala as the main medium of monastic education. Thera Dharmakirti added the first prolongation of the *Mahavamsa*, updating the Chronicle to the reign of Parakramabahu II. This king, himself, had attained distinction for his contribution to literature. In his reign the *Jataka Pota*, the most revered work of popular Buddhism, was translated into Sinhala by a committee led by a monk from Cola. The Sidatsangara, a Sinhala grammar modelled on a Tamil grammatical treatise, dealt exclusively with pure Sinhala as used in poetry of the period.

Prose narrative literature also made tremendous advances in order to keep pace with the growing public demand for books to read. Among the most reputed writers were lay scholars such as Gurulugomi and Vidyacakravarti. Their respective works, the *Amavatura* and *Dharmapradipika*, and the *Butsarana, Dahamsarana* and *Sangasarana*, are among the greatest classics of Sinhala literature, as are the works of several monks, such as the *Pujavaliya* of the Thera of Mayurapada, and the *Saddharmalankaraya* of Thera Dharmakirti, while several *Vamsakathas* were translated during this period.

Equally significant were developments in the field of Sinhala poetry, where a wide range of metres with a rhyme at the end as well as one or more intermediate places tested the mastery of the composer's language.

The Kingdom of Kotte and the golden age of Sinhala poetry

The seat of administration of Parakramabahu VI was Sri Jayavardhanapura, better known as Kotte. As in the successive capitals since the drift to the south-west, no major monuments matching the grandeur of Anuradhapura or Polonnaruva had been constructed in Kotte. This apparent decadence in art and architecture could be related to the vagaries of the economy of the island which had progressively lost its importance as a trade emporium as a result of the expansion of the Arabs to South-East Asia, thereby permitting the Chinese to trade with the West while bypassing Sri Lanka.

The reign of Parakramabahu VI was not altogether peaceful. He repelled an invasion by the ruler of Karnataka and carried out a punitive expedition against the Cola ruler who plundered a Sri Lankan ship. The Colas had to pay tribute to him for a period. At the same time he had to deal with rebellions in the central hilly region, and also mounted a successful operation, led by Sapumal Kumaraya, to bring the Kingdom of Jaffna under his suzerainty. But the reunification of Sri Lanka was short-lived, since Jaffna regained its autonomy within seventeen years.

Buddhism flourished, and several seats of higher learning actively contributed to the promotion of literature and scholarship. Both Hinduism

Lion, Yapahuva, 13th century.
A lion sculpture that reflects South East Asian characteristics

and the Tamil language were subjects earnestly studied there. Hindu gods gained in popularity among Buddhists and were worshipped in shrines close to or sometimes on the premises of Buddhist temples. Naturally, these tendencies were resisted by more orthodox monks such as Thera Vidagama Maitreya. A new type of verse literature, however, the *Sandesa*, in which birds are represented as carrying invocations to the Hindu gods, bears testimony to the growing spirit of co-existence of Buddhism and Hinduism in Buddhist society.

The reign of Parakramabahu VI was the heyday of Sinhala poetry. The *Samgharaja* Thera Totagamuve Rahula himself was an accomplished poet. To his credit stand the *Mahakavya Kavyasekharaya* and two *Sandesa* poems, of which the *Salalihini Sandesa* is a work of great literary merit. Thera Vidagama Maitreya's poems were more religious and didactic. His *Budugunalankaraya* and *Lovadasangarava* are delightful treatises on Buddhist teachings and practice in crystal-clear verse. Thera Vattave's *Guttilakavya* has been acclaimed as a gem of poetic expression. A panegyric on Parakramabahu VI, the Parakumbasirita marked a departure in style and vocabulary in Sinhala verse literature and became a model for the popular versifiers of the next two centuries. The penury of prose works of the period shows an increasing tendency towards Sanskritization.

The coming of the Portuguese and the fall of Kotte

The grandson of Parakramabahu VI was hardly two years into his reign when he was slain by Sapumal Kumaraya, who became king as Bhuvanekabahu VI. It was in his reign that Sri Lanka played a major role in restoring Buddhism in Myanmar in 1476. The Portuguese arrived in Sri Lanka in 1505 during the reign of his grandson.

The Portuguese stood to gain from the dissensions in the court of Kotte. The weak King Vijayabahu VII (1509-21) was murdered by his own three sons, who divided his kingdom among themselves. Mayadunne with Sitavaka as his capital became a threat to the eldest brother, Bhuvanekabahu of Kotte. The latter sought Portuguese help not only to secure the kingdom for himself, but also to ensure that his grandson Dharmapala succeeded him.

In an unusual display of loyalty to the Portuguese, the effigy of the young prince was sent to Portugal to be crowned by John III in 1541. Dharmapala also converted to Catholicism and was baptized as *Don Juan*. He ascended the throne in 1551, and actual power passed into the hands of the Portuguese. Christianity, as well as Western norms and customs, gained currency. With the death of Dharmapala in 1597, the Portuguese became *de juro* and *de facto* sovereigns of a sizeable part of the country.

The last shreds of independence

In the meantime, the Kingdom of Jaffna led a precarious existence vis-a-vis the Portuguese. Sangily at first allowed Catholic missionaries to operate freely in his territories, but when Saint Francis Xavier's efforts began to bear visible fruits, he turned against them. The Portuguese made an unsuccessful attempt in 1544 to avenge the massacre by Sangily of six hundred converts in Mannar. Again, when further enraged by his support of their Sinhala enemies, the Portuguese sent another punitive expedition in 1561 which was partly successful. A third expedition in 1591 resulted in the death of Sangily, although the Portuguese were still not keen to administer Jaffna directly. Their protege Sangily Kumara, however, proved less loyal than expected. He was captured in 1619 and sent to Goa. The kingdom of Jaffna ceased to exist.

The trials and tribulations of the Kingdom of Kotte were so many opportunities for the Kings of Sitavaka to make several near-successful attempts to gain supremacy. Although they could muster naval support from the Zamorin of Calicut on the Malabar coast of South India, both Mayadunne and his son Rajasimha I were finally defeated by the superior fire-power of the Portuguese.

The rise of the Kingdom of Kandy

Kandy had already become the seat of government of an independent or semi-independent ruler at least three decades before the arrival of the Portuguese. Sena Sammata (1469-1511) Vikramabahu (1471-1511) is credited with founding the city of Kandy. The hostilities of Rajasimha I of Sitavaka in particular drove a number of princes, princesses and children of chieftains to seek asylum with the Portuguese. An attempt in 1592 to put one of them on the throne under the suzerainty of the Portuguese had an unforeseen result. The commander of the successful expedition, Konappu Bandara, also baptized *Don Juan*, turned against the Portuguese and ascended the throne as Vimaladharmasuriya.

Another expedition by the Portuguese in 1594 to replace him by the daughter of an erstwhile King of Kandy was also routed. The Princess, Kusumasana Devi, or *Dona Catherina*, was captured. Reinforcing his claim to the throne by marrying her, Vimaladharmasuriya (1590-1604) founded a line of able rulers who fought off frequent attacks by the Portuguese.

Vimaladharmasuriya was the first to commence tentative negotiations with the Portuguese. His cousin, Senarat (1604-35) continued such negotiations in the face of renewed attacks by the Portuguese. He won decisive victories over Jeronimo de Azeveda (1611) and Constantino de Sa Noronha (1630). In his search for foreign sea support to outflank the Portuguese, an opportunity arose for the involvement of the Danish, who sent five warships, but these negotiations did not proceed any further.

Rajasimha II and the advent of the Dutch

Negotiations with the Dutch in the reign of Rajasimha II (1629-87), the most powerful ruler of Kandy, were more fruitful. The battle of Gannoruva in 1638 was followed by a joint operation with the Dutch to capture the Portuguese fort at Batticaloa. In the course of the following two years, the Dutch occupied Trincomalee, Negombo and Galle. A dispute over the payment of the cost of these wars enabled the Dutch to retain these forts. With the appointment of the first Dutch Governor or Commander in 1640, the Dutch rule of the occupied territories became a reality.

As the battles between the two colonial powers raged during the next two decades, Rajasimha II continued to claim that all the territories captured by the Dutch should eventually be passed on to him, but the Dutch quibbled over payment of costs and refused to part with them. With the fall of Colombo in 1656 and Mannar, Kayts and Jaffna in 1658, Portuguese rule ended in Sri Lanka. How the Sinhalas reacted to this transfer of territories from one European power to another is reflected in the saying that it was like exchanging pepper for ginger.

Rajasimha II continued to control the central hills and the east coast. He looked for other European powers to oust the Dutch and among whom were the French and the British. In his territories he gave asylum to the Portuguese who were being persecuted on both religious and political grounds. The king's support for Catholics to practise their form of Catholicism freely is exemplified by the church of Vahakotte. Robert Knox, an English prisoner, has left behind a most comprehensive account of the political, social, religious and cultural conditions of the Kingdom of Kandy in his *Historical Relation of the Island of Ceylon*, published in London in 1681.

The end of the Sinhala dynasty

Both economically and politically, the Kingdom of Kandy began to decline after Rajasimha II. With the death of his grandson, Sri Vira Parakrama Narendrasimha (1707-1739), the Sinhala dynasty ended. The throne passed to his brother-in-law, Kirti Sri Rajasimha (1747-1780). While his four queens came from Madura, his secondary wife, a Sinhala, appears to have been responsible for his pro-Buddhist policies which contributed to his popularity. His brother, Rajadhirajasimha (1780-1798) followed him as king and also died childless. Pilimatalave, the chief minister, contrived to place on the throne another Nayakkar who assumed the name of Sri Vikramarajasimha (1798-1815).

The Dutch continued to govern the coastal areas which they had acquired in the reign of Rajasimha II, but the dissatisfaction of their subjects, added to the growing popularity of Kirti Srirajasimha due to his patronage of Buddhism, culminated in a rebellion in 1760. This prompted the Dutch to invade Kandy, which they held for nine months. The war eventually ended in 1766 with the conclusion of a treaty which was grossly unfavourable to the King of Kandy. Under its terms, the entire maritime belt all around the island came under Dutch rule.

Reunification of the island under British rule

The British saw an opportunity to continue their hostilities against the Dutch and made contacts with the Nayakkar kings. In 1782 Trincomalee was taken by the British but was soon captured by the French, who held it for a year. Although it was restored to the Dutch, the British took it again in 1795. Jaffna surrendered the same year. Colombo too was taken by the British without any resistance. Thus the Dutch territories of Sri Lanka passed to the British in 1796. With the Treaty of Amiens in 1802, the maritime region of the island was confirmed as a British colony.

The British sent several expeditions, as their predecessors had done, to annex Kandy. They failed for the same reason, but because of the unpopularity of the last Nayakkar king who was described as a ruthless and cruel tyrant, the British found themselves approached by courtiers and chieftains. With their collaboration, Sri Vikrama Rajasimha was deposed and the Kingdom of Kandy was transferred to British rule in 1815 under the terms of a treaty known as the 'Kandyan Convention'. After the brief seventeen-year reign of Parakramabahu VI, the island was politically reunited. Uprisings in 1817 and 1848 fashioned the British administrative and educational policy.

A clamour for constitutional reforms arose as early as 1865. A national leadership took shape as education expanded and new professions in law, medicine and administration as well as economic opportunities in plantations and commerce were open to Sri Lankans. Progressive reforms in the legislative and executive branches of the Government to cater for the rising middle class culminated in the introduction of universal suffrage in 1931.

A territorially elected State Council was instituted with a system of executive committees, each under a minister, to address socio-economic issues vigorously. Some of the most important legislative measures pertaining, not only to such issues as health and free education but also to the fields of antiquities, research and higher education were taken by the State Council.

Independence

Within months of adopting a Constitution with far greater national autonomy, Sri Lanka became independent on 4 February 1948, remaining part of the British Commonwealth. The 1972 Constitution created the Republic and made Sri Lanka the official name in all languages.

The 1978 Constitution, with its subsequent amendments, has brought into existence a unicameral Parliament with an Executive President, a Prime Minister with a Cabinet of Ministers, and a system of Provincial Councils with specified legislative power and a Chief Minister and Board of Ministers in each Province. The current dispute with a group of Tamil militants relates to the degree of devolution of power to provincial administrations.

Religious and cultural life in the colonial period

A veritable decadence in the religious and cultural life set in with the fall of the Kingdom of Kotte. Portuguese oppression of national religions coincided with the hostilities of Rajasimha I of Sitavaka who, seeking to absolve his crime against his father, became a Hindu. Even Alagiyavanna,the last poet to hold on to the classical traditions of Sinhala literature, converted to Catholicism.

While the early kings of Kandy filled the gap with a certain measure of success and provided a ray of hope to the population of the rest of the island, the continuing wars with the Portuguese and the Dutch had a harmful effect. The destruction of temples and the disruption of the Samgha deprived the people of much-needed leadership in the areas of religion and culture.

Although war ballads and erotic folk poems became prolific at this time, it should be said that the intellectual life of the nationals of Sri Lanka was at a very low ebb. No literary works of any merit made their appearance. In art and architecture, while no spectacular works comparable with those of earlier days had been produced, national creativity was preserved by craftsmen and is reflected in the decorative motifs in court and household ornaments and furniture. The perennial gift for architectural creativity displayed in such monuments as Embekke Devalaya, the Gadaladeniya and the Lankatilaka of the fourteenth to fifteenth centuries can; however, be traced in some of the remarkable structures of the Kandyan Kingdom: notably the Inner Sanctum of the Dalada Maligawa, attributed to Vimala Dharma Surya II, and the gediges of Natha Devale and Adahanamaluva.

Equally significant is the preservation of the techniques and themes of mural painting as characterized by Sittara folk art. With the weakening of Buddhism and the corresponding increase in the propitiation of Hindu and folk divinities, popular exorcism cults such as Bali, Tovil and Devil Dancing were introduced from South India and elsewhere. With them developed related art forms in sculpture and painting, mask carving and dance, music and drama. The growing cultural impact of South India in the court brought into existence secular dance forms, now acclaimed as Kandyan Dancing, along with the musical accompaniments of Vannam and Prasasti.

Renaissance of Buddhism and its impact on culture

It is noteworthy that steps to revitalize Buddhism were actually initiated by the first two Nayakkar kings. Sri Vijayarajasimha with his queens adopted Buddhism and, according to the Mahavamsa, was the first patron of Velivita Sri Saranankara. Invitations to Arakan, Pegu and Siam to send monks to reintroduce Higher Ordination were also sent by this king with the help of the Dutch.

The mission from Siam led by Thera Upali, however, came in 1753 in the reign of Kirti Sri Rajasimha. With the guidance of Thera Velivita Sri Saranankara who had now become the Samgharaja, the Supreme Patriarch, Kirti Sri Rajasimha, ushered in a Buddhist renaissance which had wide-ranging impact on the entire cultural life of the country.

The temples he built or restored are treasure-houses of Buddhist art as exemplified by the mural paintings of Arattana near Kandy, Degaldoruva, Gangaramaya, Madavala and Suriyagoda. The influence of this art is also said to have extended to Kelaniya, Mulkirigala and Telwatta. The restoration of the murals or their replacement at Dambulla is also attributed to Kirti Sri Rajasimha. He was responsible too for the expansion of the two monastic complexes of Kandy, namely Asgiriya and Malvatta. An unusually ambitious building begun by him but not completed is Gamaduva near Kundasale. The upsurge in architectural and artistic activity during his reign is also to be observed in places like Hanguranketa where some of the finest decorative motifs in Kandyan art are preserved.

Far more far-reaching was the contribution of the Samgharaja and the king in the field of scholarship and literature. The traditional educational system was revived and teachers went from Kandy to rekindle the torch of learning in the parts of the country that were under Dutch rule. Books were recopied, libraries established and treatises, especially teaching manuals, developed. Even the third Nayakkar king contributed to the growing literature with a poem of his own, the *asa disa da kava*.

National Religions under British rule

Buddhism thrived alongside Hinduism and other folk cults, which were collectively called Devagama, the religion of gods. When the Kandyan Convention was drawn up and the British rulers were required to take over the religious responsibilities of the traditional royalty, the Sinhala version of the document referred to both the religion of the Buddha and Devagama, although the English version had, whether inadvertently or otherwise, dropped any reference to the latter. Though no specific mention was made in the Convention, both Islam and Catholicism were protected and freely practised in the Kandyan kingdom without the impediments to which their co-religionists were subjected by the Dutch.

The early years of British rule had a negative effect on national religions. As far as Buddhism was concerned, some steps were deliberate. For example, with a view to ending religious contacts with monastic establishments in Kandy, the monks in the low country were encouraged

Sangharaja being appointed by the king. A painting from Kelaniya Rajamahavihara, by Solias Mendis, early 20th century.

to seek Higher Ordination in Myanmar so as to set up their own independent sects.

What affected all religions, however, was the decision to hand over the entire educational system of the country to Protestant Christian missionaries. Evangelization was the *raison d',tre* of the schools they established. The formal closure of Buddhist temple schools in 1864 was another step in the alienation of the laity from the temple. So vigorous and effective were the efforts made jointly by the church and the administration, that even well-informed national scholars like James d'Alwis predicted that Buddhism would cease to exist in Sri Lanka by the end of the nineteenth century.

The national and religious revival movement

Apparently galvanized into action by these predictions, the Buddhists took the offensive first by issuing tracts, intensifying Buddhist scholarship and entering into open controversy with the Christian clergy. They had a band of enthusiastic and influential allies in Western orientalists who were delving into Eastern religions and literature. They were impressed with what they discovered and found the general trend of criticism and denigration unfair, if not faulty. Fortunately several of the better known scholars were associated with the administration of the island. Their support was vital to the establishment of seats of learning like the Vidyodaya (1873) and Vidyalankara (1875) Parivenas and for the publication of Pali and Sinhala classics.

Archaeological and epigraphical studies, which had hitherto been conducted on an *ad hoc* basis, came to be restructured with the formal creation of the Archaeological Survey of Ceylon in 1890 under H.C.P.Bell. Several able and devoted foreign specialists carried on his work with unabated interest until local scholars such as D.M. de Z. Wickremasinghe and Senerat Paranavitana took over. At a time when the need was greatest, these scholars restored the confidence of the people of Sri Lanka by highlighting the nation's past achievements.

The final spurt of action in the national and religious revival movement was an unexpected result of the Buddhist-Christian controversy of Panadura in 1873. Having read a report of this event in an American newspaper, Madame H.P. Blavatsky and Colonel Henry Steele Olcott, both of whom were noted Theosophists, decided to come to Sri Lanka. The latter embraced Buddhism on his arrival in 1880 and did yeoman service in ushering in a system of Buddhist education through modern schools.

This emphasis on education had a wider impact. Even the Catholics, who had hitherto been deprived of state support which was exclusively reserved for the Protestant Christian missionaries, made common cause. Leaders such as Arumuga Navalar among the Hindus and Siddi Lebbe among the Muslims campaigned for the promotion of their religious systems.

Among the Sinhalas, Anagarika Dharmapala agitated for reforms in every field, political, administrative and economic. He considered independence from foreign domination as vital to national development. Progressively, state policy was made more equitable and the twentieth century dawned with a better deal for all, even though all the problems were not solved.

From the point of view of literature and the performing arts, new influences came from various quarters. The Western novel and the short story provided prototypes and themes for Sinhala and Tamil writers. Drama, which had been more in the bleachers as folk entertainment on South Indian and Christian models, came under the influence of the modern theatre.

Historical and cultural background to the UNESCO-WFP-Sri Lanka Cultural Triangle Project

It is in the context of such an evolving and vibrant cultural background that the study of the nation's past has become an absorbing intellectual pursuit of the Sri Lankans.

Their perennial historical sense has been the source of constant motivation in the search. Yet each discovery confirming the glory and grandeur of the national heritage has stressed, on the one hand, the importance of sharing it with humanity as a whole and, on the other, the enormous responsibility of safeguarding it as the heritage of all mankind. It is in this spirit that Sri Lanka has given priority to the study and conservation of its cultural patrimony. Much has been done over the last hundred years through national initiative and resources.

The UNESCO-WFP-Sri Lanka Cultural Triangle Project is therefore an invitation to the world to share not only in enjoying but also in safeguarding a common heritage hand in hand with a nation that is proud to be its custodian.

Abhayagiri Vihara

The Northern Monastery, Anuradhapura

T. G. Kulatunga and Athula Amarasekera

An exemplary foundation

Anuradhapura, one of the most extensive ruins in the world, and one of its most sacred pilgrimage cities, was a great monastic centre as well as a royal capital, with magnificent monasteries rising to many stories, all roofed with gilt bronze or tiles of burnt clay glazed in brilliant colours. To the north of the city, encircled by great walls and containing elaborate bathing ponds, carved balustrades and moonstones, stood Abhayagiri, one of seventeen such religious units in Anuradhapura and the largest of its five major viharas. Surrounding the humped *dagaba*, Abhayagiri Vihara was a seat of the Northern Monastery, or *Uttara Vihara.*

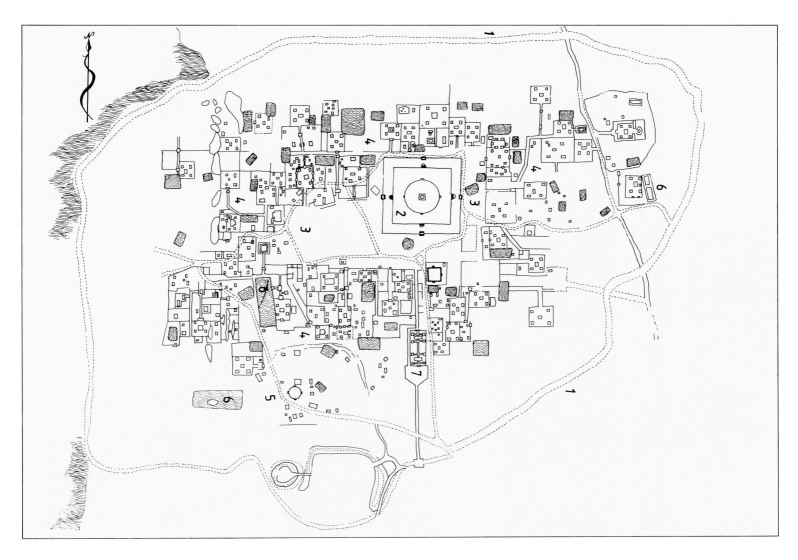

Monastery Plan, Abhayagiri
1. *Peripheral road*
2. *Stupa*
3. *Grove*
4. *Residential Courtyards*
5. *Lankarama*
6. *Baths*
7. *Modern Residence and Museum*

Classical Entrance, Abhayagiri, Anuradhapura, 6th-8th centuries.
The entrances of Sri Lankan architecture had been refined to classical perfections with decorated steps, a moonstone, balustrade and formal guardstones.

The term Abhayagiri Vihara means not only a complex of monastic buildings, but also a fraternity of Buddhist monks, or *Sangha*, which maintained its own historical records, traditions and way of life. Founded in the second century B.C., it had grown into an international institution by the first century of this era, attracting scholars from all over the world and encompassing all shades of Buddhist philosophy. Its influence can be traced to other parts of the world, through branches established elsewhere. Thus, the Abhayagiri Vihara developed as a great institution vis-a-vis the Mahavihara and the Jetavana Buddhist monastic sects in the ancient Sri Lankan capital of Anuradhapura.

Once flourishing, the great monasteries of Anuradhapura fell into melancholy ruin, only to be overgrown with vegetation, their walls and roofs pierced by the thrust of trees and tangled roots, and the great *dagaba* became a tree-covered hillock the size of a town. After many centuries of oblivion, they are again being explored and cleared, and detailed excavation and conservation work is now leading to the rediscovery of an exquisite royal city of temples and monasteries.

It is recorded in the chronicles that Abhayagiri was established by King Vattagamani Abhaya (Valagamba), during the period of his second reign, from 89 to 77 B.C. Within five months of his accession to the throne for the first time in 103 B.C., a young Brahmin named Tiya (Tissa) declared war against him. Tiya was deluded by the prophecy of another Brahmin into thinking that he was destined to become king. Before the arrival of Mahinda Thera, who brought Buddhism to the Island, Brahmins held the highest place in society. After the establishment of the *Bhikkhu* order in the island, however, they lost their supremacy, and were replaced by the Buddhist *Sangha*. Some Brahmins converted to Buddhism, while others raised the standard of revolt. Tiya, who enjoyed the support of his community, lived both in and outside of Sri Lanka, and was therefore very powerful.

At the same time, seven Tamil chiefs landed at Mahatittha with a mighty army. King Valagamba, a good diplomat, realising that his forces were too

Ruined Relic House, Abhayagiri, Anuradhapura, 5th-8th centuries. A very elegantly constructed edifice with refined details and delicate sculptures to enhance the design.

weak to fight against both of these enemies, tried to rid himself of them by making them fight each other 'like a palm leaf cutting itself'. He sent a message to Tiya that he could have the kingdom, provided he managed to defeat the foreign invaders. Tiya agreed, advanced with his forces to meet the Tamils, and was vanquished by them. The Tamils, elated by their success, advanced towards Anuradhapura and defeated the king, who was forced to abandon the throne and go into hiding in the mountains. As the King, defeated in battle, was fleeing Anuradhapura, a *Jain* priest of the Giri Monastery, which had been built by King Pandukhabaya near the northern gate of the city, cried out 'The great black Sinhala is fleeing.'

The king thereupon resolved, 'If my wish (of regaining the kingdom) is fulfilled, I will build a Temple here.'

During the period of famine and foreign rule which followed, Vattagamani Abhaya took refuge in the mountain region collecting troops until, after more than fourteen years of exile, he marched on Anuradhapura in 89 B.C., and defeated the last Tamil king, Bhatiya. In fulfilment of the vow made on the day of his defeat, one of his first acts was to build the Abhayagiri Vihara on the site of the Giri monastery. Mahatissa Thera of Kupikkala was appointed as its Chief Incumbent, as a mark of gratitude for his support in the fight against the invaders. Abhayagiri thereafter became a symbol not only of religious, but also of national resurgence, as it signaled the end of Brahmin and Jain influence in the country.

According to the chronicles, the name Abhayagiri Vihara originated from the names of King Vattagamani Abhaya and of the Giri priests who lived in the Jain monastery. However, since most ancient monasteries were built around a hillock, or *giri* in Sinhala, examples being the Vessagiri, Meghagiri or Chetiyagiri monasteries, it is possible that the name Abhayagiri symbolizes the monastery created by Vattagamani Abhaya after his recapture of the kingdom surrounding the hillock known as Digapasana, now inside the Abhayagiri complex.

Although the monastery came into being as a breakaway faction of the Mahavihara, professing the Theravada doctrine, there are, initially, no discernible differences from the Mahavihara in its attitude towards doctrine or religious practices until, according to the *Nikaya Sangraha* (the Story of the Sects), a monk called Dhammaruci, of the Vajjiputtaka sect, arrived at Abhayagiri in 77 B.C. After that time, the monks came to be known as Dhammarucis as they accepted the theory of *Puggala-attavada* of the Vajjiputtaka sect, a breakaway sect differing from the orthodox Mahavihara Buddhist sect of Anuradhapura, which had originated in India. A later attempt in the third century AD, to introduce Vaitulyavada, another school of Buddhist thought, was subsequently frustrated.

The golden age of Abhayagiri

The accession of King Mahasena in the third century A.D., saw the suppression of the Theravada doctrine practised by the Mahavihara monks. The king prohibited the giving of alms to them and went as far as to demolish the buildings of the Mahavihara and re-use their materials for the construction of new buildings at the Abhayagiri. The accession of Mahasena ushered in the golden age of Abhayagiri. After the Buddha's Tooth Relic was brought to Sri Lanka in the fourth century, Abhayagiri was selected to house the relic for public veneration.

> Fa-hsien, a Chinese monk recounts that : 'Ten days from now, Buddha's tooth will be brought out and carried to the Abhayagiri Monastery... on both sides of the road, the king sets images of the Five Hundred Forms which the Buddha assumed in his previous existence.'

By the time Fa-hsien came to Sri Lanka in search of the Dhamma, visited Abhayagiri in 412 A.D., it had developed into a leading Buddhist centre of Sri Lanka. He spent two years studying the *Dhamma* doctrine, and carried away copies of texts of the Mahayana doctrine.

'Fa-hsien stayed in this country for two years and obtained a copy of the "Rules of the Mahisasakas". He also procured copies of the "Dirgagama", the "Samyuktagama" and the "Sannipata", all of which were unknown in China.'

By the seventh century A.D., Abhayagiri Vihara consisted of four *mulas*, fraternities or grouped institutions for religious teaching: the Uttara-mula, Kapara–mula, Mahanethpa–mula and Vahadu–mula, all of which have now been located and identified through archaeological excavations, research and epigraphical evidence. In the course of time, Abhayagiri had developed into a well-organized religious and educational institution having well-established relations with China, Java and Kashmir.

According to the Chinese text *Pi-Chitu-Ni-Chung*, the biography of the *bhikkhunis* (nuns) compiled by Pao Chang in 526 A.D., and the biography of Gunavarnam and Sanghavarman, the Sinhala nuns gave the second *Upasampada*, or higher ordination, to the Chinese nuns. According to another Chinese source, in 426 A.D. eight Sinhala *(Shin-iza-kuo)* nuns *(pi-chiu-ni)* arrived in Nanking, the capital of the early Sung dynasty (420-77 A.D.), on a foreign merchant ship owned by a certain Nandi. Consequently, three more nuns, headed by *Tie-so-re* (Tissara in Sinhala), arrived in Nanking. Thus in the year 434 over three thousand nuns received their higher ordination for the second time in the presence of more than ten Sinhala nuns headed by Tissara at the Nanking Temple in China.

Residential Complex, Abhayagiri, Anuradhapura, 5th-8th centuries.
The residences as seen through the porter's lodge. The planning of the early architects was to provide a commanding view of the whole complex as one entered the premises.

It is also recorded that there were religious contacts between Sri Lanka and Java through the Abhayagiri Vihara, at least towards the end of the eighth century, as attested by a fragmentary inscription from the Ratubaka plateau in central Java. This inscription records the establishment of 'the Abhayagiri Vihara of Sinhalese ascetics trained in the sayings of *Jinas* (Buddha).' Commenting on this record, J.G. de Casparis observes, 'The most important detail is the name of the foundation, vis., the Abhayagiri Vihara. The name at once suggests that of the famous monastery of Anuradhapura, and the addition of the words "of the Sinhalese" proves that this is not just a coincidence. In fact, the foundation is a second Abhayagiri Vihara...either in common with it in form or spirit, or both, to deserve the same name.'

Periodic South Indian invasions, especially in the ninth century in the reign of Sena I, almost half a century of Cola rule and the subsequent abandonment of the capital, Anuradhapura, led to the disintegration of the Abhayagiri Vihara. Despite efforts by Vijayabahu I and Parakramabahu I in the thirteenth century to renovate and resurrect the temple, its gradual destruction in the course of time could not be averted, particularly after the final transfer of the capital from Polonnaruva in the Rajarata, or King's Country, to an alternative location in 1215 as a result of repeated *Maga* invasions.

A dark era of eight hundred years engulfed Abhayagiri Vihara until its rediscovery in the 1880s awoke scientific and scholarly interest in the abandoned and vandalized ruins. Mistakenly identified at first with Jetavana Vihara, they were photographed and drawn by specialists in the late nineteenth century, while the Department of Archaeology, established about the same period, undertook excavation and conservation work of some of the edifices at the beginning of the twentieth century.

Planning and layout

Covering approximately 200 hectares, Abhayagiri Vihara had all the components required by doctrine for a Buddhist temple; the image house, stupa, Bo Tree shrine, chapter house (*poyage* or *ruvanpaha*), residence for monks, and refectories. This is confirmed by the inscriptions of Mahinda IV (956-972 A.D.) found at Abhayagiri: 'Whatever remains after repairs have been effected,...at the site of the great stone statue, Ruvanpaha (the chapter-house) at the Abayatura-maha-sa...at the shrine of the sacred Bo Tree... shall be kept as communal property.' Recent archaeological excavations at the site have also revealed other features such as roadways, assembly halls and temple buildings such as the Abhisheka Mandapa (the ceremonial anointing hall).

A road access system anticipating modern concepts of town planning has been uncovered, with the highway from the city to the north running through the monastery. The roads and pathways, generally paralleled with the principal axes, are up to ten metres wide. Fa-hsien throws some light on the circumstances of their creation: 'Buddha's Tooth will be brought out and carried to Abhayagiri Monastery. All monks and laymen who wish to do good deeds may level the roads, adorn the lanes and streets, and prepare all kinds of flowers and incense as offerings.'

By the seventh century, the stupa, the *Uposathagara* chapter house, the refectory, the principal *Bodhighara,* and the assembly hall of the Abhayagiri fraternies were completed. The principal roadways and common water bodies were shared by the residents of thirty subsidiary monasteries composed of a quincunx of monastic residences, or *pancavasa*, within each of the four fraternities. Spatially, the public and private domains of the monasteries were clearly defined, as dictated by the doctrine. The public spaces surrounding the stupa contained the principal *Bodhighara* of the complex to the south-east, the *sannipatasala* or assembly hall, the chapter house and the Abhisheka Mandapa. The *asanaghara* can now be identified as the principal Bo Tree shrine of Abhayagiri.

The stupas

According to Fa-hsien, 'Buddha once came to this country to convert a dragon...Over the footprint north of the royal city, a great stupa, four hundred feet high, was erected...by, the side of this stupa was erected the monastery called Abhayagiri'.

The centre-piece of the monastery and its four fraternities, Abhayagiri Stupa, consisting of outer and inner terraces enclosed by walls, is over 75 metres high and 106.5 metres in diameter at its widest point. The outer terrace was strewn with sand, while the inner terrace was stone-paved. The rain-water falling on this vast stretch of land was drained into four

Prasada Stupa, Abhayagiri, Anuradhapura, 8th-9th centuries.
Stepped stupas of the prasada type are rare in Sri Lanka. This has a flight of steps designed to provide access to the upper storeys.

ponds built near the four entrances to the stupa grounds. Today stripped of parts of its outer casing and covered by vegetation, the great dome was built of solid brickwork laid in a butterclay mortar, and may contain small, inaccessible chambers or *garba* concealed in its interior. The superstructure above the dome consists of the massive rectangular cube of the *hataraskotuva* surmounted by the circular *devatakotuva* and the badly deteriorated spire.

The stupa as it stands today is the original as last renovated by Parakramabahu I. No major renovation or conservation has been done since, apart from some attempts at consolidation of the cube, cylinder and spire by the Department of Archaeology in 1910-12 and reconstruction of parts of the three basal terraces by the chief monks in 1926 and after. J. G. Smither attempted a careful documentation and after which he published in the form of several excellent drawings in his monumental book, 'Archaeological Remains, Anuradhapura, Ceylon', in 1884.

There are other stupas in the Abhayagiri Vihara complex. One such is the Lankarama Stupa which originally had a conical roof covering. This has been identified as the Silasobbhakandaka Cetiya built by King Valagamba. Another tall brick structure, situated in Vahadu-mula to the west of the Elephant Pond, was previously thought to be a library building, but turned out to be a stupa. Yet another, popularly known as Indikatu Seya, is situated close to the Ratnaprasada. The last two stupas are similar in design to the well-known Naka Vehera. The Indikatusaye, or Needle Stupa, is an example of the ingenuity of the ancient Sinhalese in planning and erecting buildings in harmony with the surrounding landscape. Stylistically, it is considered to be Mahayanic.

The Bo Tree shrine

'A former king of this country', relates Fa-hsien, 'had sent a messenger to the middle kingdom to fetch a seed of the *Pattra* tree to plant beside the hall, and this grew some two hundred feet high. This tree inclined towards the south-east and, fearing that it might fall, the king set up a huge pillar that required eight or nine men to encircle it, to support the tree. At the place where the tree was propped, a branch grew from the trunk and pierced the pillar, then sent down roots to the ground. This branch was so thick that it took four men to encircle it. Though the pillar is cleft in two, since it still supports the tree, it has not been removed. Under this tree is a rest house containing a seated image of the Buddha to which both monks and laymen pay homage continuously.' The *Pattra* tree mentioned by Fa-hsien is the Bo-Tree at Buddha-Gaya in India where Buddha achieved enlightenment.

From previous excavations by the Archaeological Department and recent excavations by the Cultural Triangle, it is now possible to identify the location of the Bodhi Tree described by Fa-hsien – the principal Bo-Tree shrine of the complex – with the monument popularly known as the *Asanaghara*, or Coronation Point. From Fa-hsien's description and the chronicles, we know that monasteries already existed by the fifth century to the south west of the stupa. It is therefore clear that, although this was the oldest Bodhi Tree of the Abhayagiri complex, it was not the first on

Abhayagiri Stupa, Anuradhapura, 1st century B.C., and after.
This is the tallest brick edifice of the ancient world originally about 350 feet high.

Bo-tree Shrine, Abhayagiri, Anuradhapura, Circa 1st-8th centuries.
This excavated site displays many phases of constructional activities the earliest being attributed to the formation of the vihara in the 1st century B.C.

the *Asanaghara*. Excavations carried out in 1962 and 1963 by Dr Godakumbura revealed three successive cultural phases. Recent excavations in the Cultural Triangle have identified a fourth stratum demarcating the trough used to plant the Bo-Tree. An inscription, dating from between the first century B.C. and the first century A.D., found in this layer, firmly establishes that the Bo-Tree shrine and the earliest refectory belong to the fourth cultural phase. Also found in the *Bodhighara* among objects of worship were representations of the footprints of the Buddha, *asana* (seats) and seated Buddha images. With the development of the Buddha statue, one can identify the use of disused footprints as column bases. Further excavations have uncovered several seated images, indicating the final development as a shrine with seated Buddhas and *asanas*.

The Image House and other monuments

'By the side of this stupa, a monastery was erected which is called Abhayagiri (the Hill of Fearlessness), and here are five thousand monks. It contains a hall for the worship of Buddha, engraved with gold and silver and adorned with precious stones. In it stands an image of Buddha made of green jade, some twenty feet high. The entire image sparkles with the seven precious substances, and its splendour and magnificence defy description. In its right hand, the image holds a priceless pearl...'

This description by Fa-hsien, and an inscription by Kasyapa V, confirm the existence of a principal Image House which it has not yet been possible to locate, although many image houses can be identified within the existing ruins. The Mahasena pavilion and the queen's pavilion, for example, indicate the existence of image houses within a *pancavasa* complex.

The largest preaching hall hitherto discovered in Sri Lanka, the *Sannipatasala,* is situated opposite the southern entrance to the Stupa, serving both the clergy and laity: this was an open hall with stone parapet walls on four sides. The entrances, facing the cardinal points, were flanked by the four guardian deities. The statue of Virupaksa, the guardian deity

Seated Buddha, Abhayagiri, Anuradhapura,
6th-8th centuries.
The image is situated at the site of an ancient
Bodhi-tree shrine.

of the west, found in ruined state, is now preserved in the Abhayagiri museum. The stone plinths of statues of other gods were also found here. The ruins of an image house towards the north-east can be dated to the late Anuradhapura period, although the remains of brick walls dating from three earlier construction phases were discovered during excavations.

The remains of a building to the south of the Ratnaprasada, the Chapter House of Abhayagiri, mistakenly thought by earlier scholars to be a refectory, were identified by Dr Roland Silva as a preaching hall. Subsequent excavations under the Cultural Triangle project at Abhayagiri have confirmed this identification.

The Abhishaka Mandapaya, or Anointing Hall, is thought to have been used for anointing Buddha statues and other objects of veneration during festivals.

The residential quarters

A *pancavasa* complex, of which approximately thirty have been found at Abhayagiri, consists of a group of five two-storied residential buildings enclosed by a wall, according to the requirements of the disciplinary code of monks, with its entrance situated at the end of an axial avenue. In its outer precincts were anciliary and service buildings. The central unit was the space for the teacher and his classroom, the upper floor being used as a library, while the four corner buildings were set aside for the pupils with three on each floor, giving a basic unit of twenty-four students to one teacher for each *pancavasa* complex. There is evidence to suggest that an image was kept within the central building. The buildings had elaborate doorways and a lotus petal pedestal of brick or stone. The walls were of brick plastered with lime mortar and reinforced with structural stone columns, while the upper floors were of timber, sometimes finished with lime plaster. The roofs of the residential buildings were covered with terra cotta roofing tiles; recent excavations have led to the discovery of ten different colours of glazed tile used to decorate the roofs.

Each of these residential units had baths, sometimes equipped for hot water, urinals and sanitary closets. The drainage system was similar to modern concepts in sanitation, and the lavatories were connected by stone conduits to septic tanks outside the building. The sanitary complex of Vahadumula is 19.75 by 13 metres and is surrounded by a brick wall. The waste water from the basin is drained by an underground conduit to a covered square soakaway pit, 2.2 metres square and of an equal depth, situated within the walled enclosure. In the centre of the stone slab covering the pit is a small circular opening, perhaps meant as an air-vent. The lavatory and ablutions adjoin each other. Within the complex, but outside the courtyard enclosure, was an area for sun-bathing after applying a medicated oil or ointment to the body. A beautifully-made urinal carved in stone, a stone seat and a paved bathroom floor have been unearthed in a *pancavasa*, behind the second *Samadhi* Buddha statue. The foul water was filtered and drained into the ground through a series of clay pots.

A small refectory comprising a kitchen and a storage area was found at the entrance to the *pancavasa* complex. This individual refectory was used for every-day meals and the daily delivery of alms.

A significant architectural feature of each complex, adding much to the beauty of the landscape environment, was the pond, often very ornamental, to which surface water was systematically drained. Other reservoirs such as the Eth Pokuna, or Elephant Pond, were linked to these smaller ponds by underground pipes.

*Residenace of a Chief Monk, Abhayagiri,
Anuradhapura, 5th-8th centuries.
The residence of a chief monk was also the
teaching unit where the pupils were guided in
their academic and religious training.*

*Urinal Stone, Abahayagiri, Anuradhapura,
6th-8th centuries.
This urinal stone is a an elaborately decorated
and exceptional piece. The fact that it was used
was evident from the soakage pots found below
the urinal trough.*

Residential Complex, Abhayagiri,
Anuradhapura, 8th-9th centuries.
The residences were all laid out as a quincunx
with the central unit for the chief monk and the
four surrounding buildings for pupils.

The biggest rice-bowl in the world

The Chinese monk Fa-hsien, who lived at Abhayagiri for nearly two years, reports that there were five thousand monks living there at that time. Within the refectory excavated and conserved by the Cultural Triangle project is a stone trough with a capacity of five thousand alms bowls, indicating that this trough was used to contain boiled rice, or alternatively, to store uncooked rice offered as alms to the *bhikkhus*. The plan of this refectory differs somewhat from those found in other monasteries in Anuradhapura. Two courtyards, paved and well-drained, ensured adequate light and ventilation to the building. There are indications that it was expanded a number of times. This is confirmed by excavated remains from four different cultural phases, and a stone inscription from the first century B.C., to the first century A.D., describing a gift to the refectory. Underground stone conduits supplied fresh water and drained away waste water. A stone sun-dial was used to ensure that the midday meal was served prior to noon, as dictated by doctrine. Hearths and various forms of grinding stones have also been found.

Ancient water management

The Elephant Pond, equivalent in area to six modern Olympic swimming pools, is perhaps the largest man-made pond in Sri Lanka. A flight of

steps leads down to the pond from the centre of each side wall. To the
north and south, underground water conduits have been found which
probably supplied water from neighbouring tanks. One such conduit
continues to function during the rainy season even today. The existence
of the *bisokotuva*, or cistern sluice, in the south-west corner, indicates
that water was distributed through conduits to other ponds in the vicinity,
and an underground conduit supplying water to the refectory to the east
has been discovered. The Elephant Pond was perhaps built fot the supply
and storage of water to three of the fraternities, excepting Kaparamula. It
is an eloquent testimony to the highly developed water management and
hydrological engineering techniques of the ancient Sinhalese.

Twin Ponds, Abhayagiri, Anuradhapura,
6th-8th centuries.
A beautiful and unusual design of two baths
joined to form a single bathing complex.

*Naga Symbol, Abhayagiri, Anuradhapura,
6th-8th centuries.*
*This symbol is generally associated with water
and is often found at water inlets or outlets.
The present example is from the Twin Ponds
complex.*

Among the most significant artistic achievements in the field of
hydrological engineering are the Twin Ponds, or Kuttam Pokuna. These
can be considered one of the outstanding architectural and artistic
creations of the ancient Sinhalese. Built of polished stone slabs, they
have entrance steps flanked by two stone *punkalas*, or pots of
abundance. The embankments were perhaps made to enable the monks
to bathe using pots or other utensils. Water supplied through the
underground conduits was first conveyed to stone chambers, or silt traps,
from whence it was filtered before flowing into the ponds. An opening
for an outlet allowing water to be drained away during repair was
discovered at the bottom of each pond. The ponds were restored during

the time of Dr Senerath Paranavitana. During excavation, small figures including a fish, a tortoise, a conch, a crab and a dancing woman were found at the bottom.

Ancient technology

The 500-acre site also contains many ancillary buildings connected with the day-to-day functioning of the monastery complex. These include foundries and workshop areas for the processing of lime plaster and pottery glazes. Samples of plaster produced in these workshops can be seen in the *vahalkada* of the stupa. The raw materials for the glazes, used for application to roofing tiles and ceramics, seem to have been lime and sand, Remnants of grinding stones, lime and sand, moulds and pots discovered at the site of the workshop building provide clues to the manufacturing process of glazes. Among several foundries which have been excavated are furnaces of clay, lined with mica and graphite. A crucible was found on one site. A gilt bronze Buddha statue, fragments of two other figures, and a bronze *astamangala* bowl with eight auspicious symbols unearthed nearby indicate that they were cast at this particular foundry. Raw materials for iron manufacture and iron slag have also been discovered, and further excavations have revealed a series of moulds for casting images, coins and crucibles.

It is significant that remnants of paintings belonging to the Anuradhapura period have been discovered in the Abhayagiri Vihara Complex. Some of these are found in the sculptures of the gateways and the gate houses. A patch of paint is found under the right shoulder of the *samadhi* Buddha statue. There is evidence in the chronicles, supported by finds from the excavations, that the entire stupa, stone slabs and statues had all been painted with locally produced lime or lime-based paint. One such 'paint factory' has in fact been discovered and restored at Abhayagiri, within the precincts of the Mahanetpamula.

Ath Pokuna or Elephant Pond, Abhayagiri, Anuradhapura, 4th-6th centuries.
This is a colossal bathing pool as it measures the equivalent of six standard Olympic pools. Documentary records indicate that there were 5,000 monks at Abhayagiri.

*Nagaraja, Abhayagiri, Anuradhapura,
5th-8th centuries.*
*The detail of the Nagaraja at the Ratnapasada
building at Abhayagiri is one of the finest
examples of an entrance guardstone.*

Architectural decoration

The architectural elements of the buildings excavated at Abhayagiri Vihara
clearly reflect the social beliefs and religious practices prevalent at the
time. Although Buddhism was the state religion, and the principle doctrine
followed by the majority of the population, the influence of other local
beliefs, particularly Hinduism, was considerable, and is expressed in the
architecture of the period. The design of entrances, for example, illustrates
the practice of placing buildings under the protection of a guardian deity.

The two slabs erected on either side of the foot of the flight of steps
leading to a building are know as guardstones. They are usually carved,
although plain guard stones have also been found. Among the Hindu
symbols represented on these stones, the most common, apart from the
Pot of Abundance and Kalpavrksa, is the figure of the *Nagaraja*, or
anthropomorphic King Cobra. The best example of these, and one of the
finest guardstones yet discovered, was found at the Ratnaprasada in
Abhayagiriya, and illustrates the degree of perfection reached by the
sculptors of Abhayagiri. Lotuses and *punkalas* are indicative of plenty.
Representations of the lotus are of particular significance in agricultural
societies where they symbolize the daughters of the guardian deity of
rain. The elephant figure at the Eth Pokuna is also a symbol of water.

The principal Buddhist guardian deities are frequently indicated by the animal vehicles of the particular gods, particularly on the guardstones. A good example is furnished by the exquisite statues on either side of the entrance to Abhayagiri Stupa. The head-dress of one of the statues is a conch while that of the other is a lotus. Representing Sanka and Padma, the two principal treasure houses of Kuvera, they are believed to have been erected to ward off any evil or danger that might threaten the stupa or its precinct. Even at present they are commonly believed to be endowed with mystic powers, and courts of law in Anuradhapura accept swearing before the statues as evidence in settlement of minor disputes between litigants.

The best example of a moonstone, a unique creation of Sri Lanka sculptors, can be seen at the foot of the steps leading to the *Pancavasa* commonly known as Mahasena's palace. A smaller example, just as exquisitely carved, was found nearby at the Queen's Pavilion. Varying in shape and size and made of different kinds of stones, all are exquisite artistic creations. According to Paranavitana, the moonstone symbolizes *samsara*, the endless cycle of rebirth, and the path to freedom from the samsaric process leading to nirvana. He interprets the pattern of the outermost ring as flames, and the various animals shown in the other concentric circles as successive phases of man's passage through *samsara*.

Moonstone, Abhayagiri, Anuradhapura, 6th-8th centuries.
This is one of the most exquisite moonstones found in Sri Lanka.

Samadhi Buddha Image, Abhayagiri,
Anuradhapura, 3rd-5th centuries.
This image is counted among the finest Buddha
figures sculptured in Sri Lanka.

The Samadhi Buddha images

The image of Buddha in *samadhi* posture, considered the finest *samadhi* image in all Sri Lanka, is dated by Coomaraswamy to a period before the third century A.D. Javaharlal Nehru wrote that he found solace during his imprisonment by the British by looking at a photograph of this statue. Sculptured out of dolomite, it is Gupta in style and execution. Probably the eyes were originally studded with gems, and a path of paint found under the right shoulder is evidence that the entire figure may have been painted. The discovery of a pit behind the statue suggests that this was one of four that stood on each side of a *Bodhigara*, or Bo-Tree shrine.

Some remarkable finds

The Ardhanarinatesvera bronze image, discovered during excavations of the inner boundary wall of the Abhayagiri Stupa, is the first of its kind discovered in the world. The dancing posture is a feature which is not found in similar statues discovered in India. Traditionally, the female half of the statue is on the left side and the male half on the right, but in this statue the opposite is the case. The male figure wears a headdress, and his left forearm is in the form of a snake's tail, the rest of the arm being in the *katakamudra*. The left leg is raised in dancing posture. The right leg, in a similar posture, is kept on the ground. The right hands have jewellery, whereas the left hands are without them. The right ear is adorned with a large and beautiful ear ornament, but the one in the left ear is not as beautiful. Each half is appropriately dressed according to its sex. This great work of art portrays the Hindu creation myth of the genesis of the human race by Agni and Soma, the principles of heat and cold.

A bronze bowl, discovered at the foundry of Mahanet - pamula, though described as a bowl, is more like a vessel with three legs. Measuring 14.5 cm., in diameter and 8 cm., in height, it is the only vessel of its kind to have been discovered in Sri Lanka. It is well-preserved and there is evidence to show that it originally bore a lid. A metal sheet fixed inside the bowl with three nails shows that it was broken into pieces. Perhaps it had been brought to the foundry for repairs.

Coins, Abhayagiri, Sri Lanka, 12th century. A most elegant design formed of symbols, letters and human forms.

Moulded in low relief in a band around the outside of the bowl are the 'eight auspicious symbols'. These are the *bhadrapita* (auspicious seat), the *matsya yugala* (double fish), the *ankusa* (elephant goad), the *camara* (fly-whisk), the *srivatsa* or *purnaghata* (pot of abundance), the *sankha* (conch), and the *svastika*. There can be no doubt that this vessel was used for ritual purposes.

Epigraphy

Over seventy inscriptions, dating from the first century B.C., to the eleventh century A.D., illustrate the development of early Brahimi, middle Sinhala, Sanskrit and Tamil. They are of inestimable value to archaeologists and historians for the new light they shed on the religious, political and socio-economic life of ancient Sri Lanka. For example, the Digapasana inscription indicates a gift to a Tamil monk by Tamil devotees. One of these inscriptions, on a paving stone in the terrace near the south frontispiece *(vahalkada)* of the stupa, helped to clear the confusion regarding the identity of Abhayagiri and Jetavana. Three important inscriptions belonging to the reigns of Mahinda IV and Kasyapa V describe the plan of the Abhayagiri complex and its administrative organization. Equally important is the discovery of a unique Sanskrit inscription at Kaparamula, which provides the exact date and time of a solar eclipse.

Ceremonial Bowl, Abhayagiri, Anuradhapura, 8th-10th centuries. A bronze bowl with the eight auspicious symbols.

Also of special significance is the finding of an inscription on a gold ingot with older lettering specifying its weight, thereby making possible a comparison between early units of measurement and those used today. Coins found at Abhayagiri date from the pre-Christian era to the Dutch period.

Ardhanarinatesvera figure, Abhayagiri,
Anuradhapura, 8th-9th centuries.
A composite male and female dancing figure
representing the Hindu God, Siva as a
manifestation of the male-female principle.

Jetavana

Stupa and monastery complex

Hema Ratnayake

Jetavanaramaya, or Jetavana Monastery, was founded by King Mahasena (276-303 A.D.), the first of the great tank builders in Sri Lanka. Historically, Jetavanaramaya is very important in the development of the three Theravadi sects in Sri Lanka. In the centre of the monastic complex stands the gigantic stupa on a square platform eight acres in extent, the largest and tallest brick-built monument in the world. When it stood in its pristine glory as a massive white structure, it was a little over 120 metres in height. This vast edifice, which has withstood the ravages of time and the elements for about 1,600 years, is an eloquent witness to the engineering expertise and

Jetavana Stupa, Anuradhapura,
3rd-4th centuries and after.
The superstructure of the stupa has collapsed.
If this was extended to its logical peak, the total
height of the stupa from the terrace would
measure about 400 feet.

the sound knowledge of geometry and physics of the ancient inhabitants of Sri Lanka. The present monastery complex is the result of gradual expansion during at least six centuries subsequent to its founding. In its present ruined state, the complex covers an area approximately 80 hectares in extent. Situated immediately to the south-east of the Citadel of Anuradhapura, its present boundaries are the Malvatu Oya to the east and south, the Halpan Ela in the west, and a road in the north.

The area where the Jetavana monastery stands was originally known as the Nandana Pleasure Grove, mentioned for the first time in connection with Thera Mahinda, the son of Emperor Asoka, the renowned ruler of India of the third century B.C. It was in the Pleasure Garden that Saint Mahinda preached the essence of the Buddha's teachings daily for seven days, bringing about the realization of the Dhamma to 7,000 people within this short period. From then on, the Nandana Grove received the honorific title of *Jotivana*, being the place from which 'the holy one had made the true doctrine shine forth', or 'the centre from which the radiance of the Dispensation became manifest.' Thera Mahinda himself is called *Dipajotaka* or 'Light of Lanka', thus establishing a close association between the great Thera and *Jotivana*, the Pleasure Grove. The name Jetavana is derived from the original Pali term, *Jotivana*. This area, directly associated with Mahinda, also came to be known as Theranambaddha Malaka, or the 'enclosure of the great Thera'. It was here that Thera Mahinda and his associate Arahats were cremated after their death. Hence, it came to be known as *Isibhumangana*.

The next occasion that we hear of Jotivana in the Pali Chronicles is in the reign of Mahasena (276-303 A.D.), whose name is associated with the appearance of a dissident sect known as Sagaliya or Jetavanavasins in Indian records, and Denamaka in Sinhala literary sources and epigraphs, at Jetavanaramaya. It is said that the king, who challenged the authority of the Mahavihara, which claimed to be the custodian of the original teachings of the Master, donated the new vihara to a Thera called Tissa, who was expelled from the priesthood. His followers settled at the new monastery under a new Thera, Sagala, and the new sect came into being. It is important to stress that these sects belong to the Theravada tradition, and that the basis of their breakaway was a difference in interpretation of the Rules of Discipline laid down by the Buddha, not the Teaching itself.

Mahinda's last resting place

The two Chronicles are vague and at variance regarding the exact identity of the spot where Thera Mahinda's body was cremated after it was brought from Mihintale, where his *parinibbana* took place. Although the same Chronicles state that King Uttiya, the brother and successor of Devanampiya Tissa, built a stupa enshrining part of the relics of Thera Mahinda on the spot where the cremation took place, the location is not clearly stated. On the other hand, more details are given regarding the place where the body of Thera Sanghamitta was cremated and a stupa built to mark the spot, that is, to the east of the Thuparama, near the Cittasala, in sight of the great Bodhi tree, which was close to the eastern gate of the Mahameghavana, having been brought through the southern gate of the city. Both sources agree that the bier of Thera Mahinda was placed in the Panhambamalaka, a spot between the Uposatha-hall and Refectory in the north-south axis, within the Mahavihara boundaries.

After due homage was paid, the bier with the Thera's body was made to circumambulate the great Thupa, Thuparama, and was cremated at a place towards the east of the Tissarama, the arama of Mahinda, according to the Dipavamsa, the older chronicle. The townsfolk who participated in the cremation ceremonies came through the eastern gate of the city. The Mahavamsa account of the event does not mention Thuparama at all. It says the monarch 'built up towards the east, in the Theranambaddha Malaka, a funeral pyre of sweet-smelling wood, leaving the Great Thupa on the right, and when he had brought the beautiful bier thither and caused it to be set upon the pyre, he carried out the rites of the dead...and here did he build a cetiya when he had caused the relics to be gathered together. Taking the half of the relics, the monarch caused thupas to be built on the Cetiya-mountain and in all viharas. The place where the burial of the sage's body had taken place is called, to do him honour, Isibhumangana, that is, the Courtyard of the Sage.'

The Stupa, or Dagaba as it is called in Sinhala, is an integral feature in any Buddhist Monastery, whether in Sri Lanka or in other Buddhist countries in South and South-East Asia. All stupas, including those built during modern times, are supposed to contain even a small particle of the corporeal remains of the Buddha or a Buddhist saint. Stupas were also built at sites where important events connected with religion took place. Yet there is no reference in the chronicles or literature whatsoever, to any commemorative edifice in this place in the Nandana Grove, in spite of it receiving the new name Jotivana, meaning the centre whence 'the radiance of the Dispensation became manifest', and which in turn earned for Mahinda the honorifics: 'Light of Lanka' and 'Anu Buddha'. Neither is there any indication as to why this spot was chosen by Mahasena, in an area claimed by Mahavihara, thereby starting another dispute with the orthodox establishment which claimed to be the custodians of the pure Theravada tradition. It is only in the thirteenth century A.D., that literary works mention that a portion of Buddha's girdle, obtained under miraculous circumstances, is enshrined there.

Recent excavations by the author under the Cultural Triangle Project in the Salapatala Maluva, a stone-paved upper terrace to the south of the Stupa, have brought to light the remains of a one-metre thick wall with an adjacent layer of ash and charcoal. The dating of several samples of bricks from the base of this wall dates it to the middle of the third century B.C. This could therefore well be the boundary wall of the Therabaddhamalaka. Current excavations have also brought to light irrefutable evidence that there were a number of small stupas belonging to the pre-Mahasena period within the Jetavanaramaya complex. If we accept the above identification, Mahasena would have built the largest stupa in the world in the Theranambaddha Malaka, which was later named Isibhumangana, again in honour of Thera Mahinda. If so, Jetavanaramaya is one of the most important religious edifices in Sri Lanka.

Jetavana Stupa, Anuradhapura,
3rd–4th centuries and after.
The super structure of the stupa has collapsed.
If this was extended to its logical peak, the total
height of the stupa from the terrace measures
about 400 feet.

Relic House, Jetavana, Anuradhapura,
6th–8th centuries.
The circular and storeyed relic house probably
displayed the golden Prajnaparamita Sutta
book found a few metres to the west of it buried
in the ground for protection.

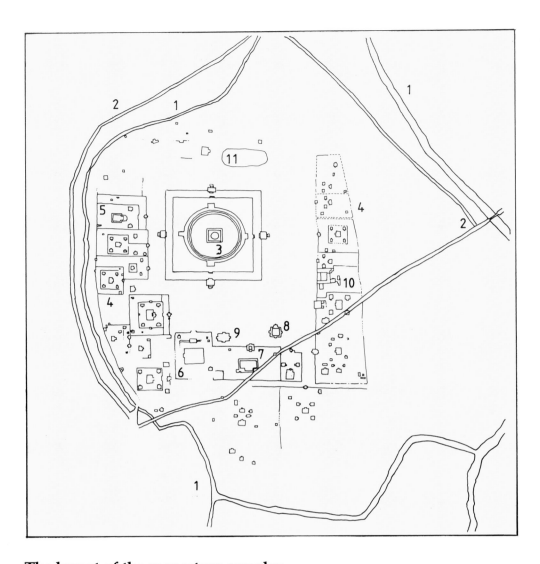

The layout of the monastery complex

The layout of this religious complex was similar to that of Abhayagiri but on a smaller scale, with about 3,000 monks when worked out on the basis of the use of the refectory. The area of the compound also covers about 48 hectares. Although the religious buildings, the community units and the residential courts are more or less identical to those of Abhayagiri, the foundation of the vihara is later, dating from the third century A.D. The position of the stupa is identical to that at Abhayagiri or for that matter any of the five major monasteries at Anuradhapura.

The site, covering approximately eighty hectares and set out as a monastery, contains all the major elements of a highly evolved monastic architecture: the *caitya* or stupa, the *pilimage* or image house, the *Bodhigara* or Bo-tree shrine, the *uposathaghara* or chapter house, the *Sannipatasala* or assembly hall, and the *pannasala* or residential complex. Also scattered around the site are many residential complexes or colleges, where pupils lived and were instructed in the different aspects of the doctrine by scholars and professor monks, and many other buildings of varying size, the purpose of which has not yet been identified.

The elements of the monastery complex are evenly disposed around the stupa and are set out in relation to the cardinal points in the following manner: the Pilimage to the west, with its entrance orientated towards the

Residential Complex, Jetavana, Anuradhapura, 9th–10th centuries.
This was probably the residence of the chief monk of the vihara, designed in the classical layout of a residential complex.

east, the Bodhigara and Uposathagara to the south, and the Danasala to the east. The residential colleges form a belt around the main stupa with their main entrances facing it, with access to and from the open terrace separating the stupa from the residential complex.

The ruins visible today above ground level belong to the last cultural phase of the site: the ninth to tenth centuries A.D. The gradual evolution of the whole monastery complex commenced at the northern end of the site in the latter half of the third century A.D., with the stupa as its focal point, gradually spreading to the north-west, south and east over a period of about six centuries. While the earlier constructions were of brick, stone came into vogue as a building material during the later centuries, and even some of the older brick buildings were enlarged using this new material.

The monastery unit seen to the south-west of Jetavana Stupa can be considered a good example of a typical *pancavasa* or 'five-unit' individual monastery. The original building of this unit stretches back to the days of the foundation of the Jetavana Vihara in the last quarter of the third century A.D., the later additions and alterations date from the tenth century.

Archaeological excavations at the site have revealed that the vast area demarcated by the massive brick boundary wall originally contained other buildings apart from the usual group of five. The main entrance to the complex faces east.

During the second phase of development, new units were added to the north-east, south-east and south-west, as well as a central *pancavasa* enclosed by a brick wall. It was during the same building phase that a well was added in the shape of a lotus leaf with steps to reach the water level. The ruined pillared hall to the south-east is probably from the same building phase.

The central 'five-unit' complex underwent development during the last phase ending in the Cola occupation of Anuradhapura in the tenth century A.D. Its central unit is unusually large, and the new stone-work on it has come to an abrupt end, leaving the carvings and finishings of the balustrades and risers uncompleted. One such example is an unfinished guardstone found very close to the building. Undoubtedly one of the best guard-stones so far found in the country, it is in a flawless state of conservation. The *Nagaraja* guardian represented in this stone is vibrant with life and vigour, and appears to be about to walk out of the rock.

The circular building to the south-west, the purpose of which is not yet fully understood, also belongs to this phase, as do the thick boundary walls.

The stone doorway of the side entrance facing the east is not only very impressive but also gives a very clear indication as to the original height of the boundary walls which once encompassed the *pancavasas*.

The tallest stupa in the world

The focal point of the monastery complex, and its most striking feature, is the Jetavana Stupa. At the time of the collapse of the Roman empire in the fourth century A.D., this was the third tallest monument in the world, being surpassed only by the two tallest pyramids at Gizeh. At over 120 metres in height, it is the tallest stupa in the world, and indeed the tallest brick building ever completed by man, containing approximately 93,300,000 baked bricks. The religious symbolism and the technical achievements of this extraordinary edifice are of international appeal and a study fascinating to man.

Plan, Jetavana Stupa
1. *Entrance*
2. *Outer Sand Court*
3. *Stone Terrace*
4. *Flower Alters*
5. *Stupa*

The whole sacred area, covering approximately 5.6 hectares, is clearly demarcated by the massive dressed stone boundary wall, which in its original form may have been about 2.4 metres high. In the centre of each side was a doorway flanked on each side by four rooms where the monks looking after the stupa and performing the religious rites at the edifice would have stayed. A sand court lay between the inner terrace and the outer wall. The terrace of the stupa was elevated about 2.4 metres; a decorated brick wall retained the earth of the terrace including the stone paving in this area. This terrace wall was originally elegantly decorated with elephant frontals and pilasters.

The stupa, accurately set out on a north-south, east-west axis, has an outer retaining wall with four *vahalkadas* or gateways, leading to a *valimaluva* or sand terrace, an inner retaining wall and *hastivedi* (elephant frieze), access steps, four *ayakas* or altars. The stupa, or *cetiya*, consists mainly of the raised square platform with flights of stairs at the four cardinal points; the three *pesa-valalu*, or basal rings of three receding stages; the dome, the *hataraskotuva*, which is the cube resting on the dome, and a cylindrical member which supports the *kotkaralla*, or pinnacle. In Sri Lanka, the architectural component above the *hataraskotuva* underwent a great evolution in its form, and probably in its significance. The present pinnacle of the Jetavana Stupa is a nineteenth-century restoration.

The building of a stupa was accompanied by elaborate ceremony. An account in the *Mahavamsa* of the building of the giant Ruvanvali Stupa at Anuradhapura, describes how the site was consolidated with broken pebbles stamped down by elephants whose feet were bound by leather. Above this were laid layers of iron mesh, mountain crystal and sheets of silver, with intervening layers of butter clay brought from faraway places. The king then 'commanded that the pure turning staff, made of silver and secured (by means of a rope) to a post of gold, be grasped by a minister of noble birth, well-attired and in festival array, and, being resolved to allot a great space for the cetiya, he ordered him to walk round (with the turning staff in his hands) along the ground already prepared.' It will be seen later how excavations have once again confirmed the accuracy of the chronicle accounts.

Excavations to the north, south and east of the base of Jetavana Stupa firmly establish the fact that the six-metre deep foundation stands on bed-rock. The stupa proper was built on a cylindrical brick base with a slight batter coming up to ground level. The original bricks when exposed suggested workmanship of fine quality and a high level of building technology. The original third century A.D., courses are strong and in good condition. The base of the stupa sits on a larger brick platform that is about 7.5 metres wider than the dome, and this in turn sits on yet another platform that extends about the same distance outward. This last platform rests on bed-rock; the uneven surface of the rock was levelled with clay. The depth of the foundation at the northern and the eastern sides is as much as 8.5 metres below the paving. The three basal terraces and the four *vahalkada* altars facing the cardinal points also rest on this brick platform, which is covered by the stone paving.

In the *Mahavamsa* account, when King Dutthagamani asks the master builder of the Ruvanvali Stupa, 'In what form wilt thou make the cetiya?', the latter 'had had a golden bowl filled with water, took water in his hand and let it fall on the surface of the water. A great bubble rose up like unto a half-globe of crystal. "Thus will I make it", he said.' The dome is indeed a very special design. Its shape has evolved, in our opinion, to a perfect mathematical equation which if extended to its logical mirror image forms a perfect spheroid comparable to those of the universe. It can also be proved that this product of bricks and clay mortar and its various angles of repose are all a by-product of many centuries of experimentation with full-scale construction; a design product of inductive logic, or an outcome of the tests of time through 'trial and error'.

The Mahavamsa again has King Dutthagamini expressing pleasure that his master builder is using a mortar of sand pounded in a mortar, sifted and finally crushed in a mill in small quantities, because 'there will be no grass or any other thing on our cetiya.' The brickwork at Jetavana is set in a perpetually pliable clay mortar which has been applied as a slurry referred

Superstructure of the Stupa, Jetavana, Anuradhapura, 3rd-4th centuries and after. The much damaged superstructure is clearly seen. Some of these elements were conserved at the turn of the century. The design of this is mainly derived from a 12th century repair by Parakramabahu I. (overleaf)

to in the ancient texts as butter clay (*navanitamattika*). This method of using a slurry is critical to providing the right homogeneity of the product where the bricks sit one upon another rather than a mortar joint. Thus the load of brick upon brick provided the right bond and the medium for load transmission from one horizontal course to another. The strength of these bricks, achieved by using conditioned clay with the right sieved mix of graded sand, resulted in these monuments standing up to its own dead load and many centuries of weathering. The strong concrete-like plaster of the surface of the dome protected the mass of bricks from direct erosion of the outside by the water run-off down the immense surface of the brickwork.

The cube, or *hataraskotuva*, of the superstructure is reminiscent of the square fence that originally stood over a burial mound. This protected the many umbrellas of honour that symbolically stood over the ashes or relics. The final design was the consolidation of the fence in massive brick masonry and the outcome was a cube with only the markings of the original upon the plaster-work. It is for this reason that it is still called the *Hataraskotuva*. In the same way the cylinder of the superstructure represents the stem of the umbrellas which had to be adequately strengthened with a stone yupa inside it to support the solidified series of umbrellas that stood above. The circular form was later associated with directional deities facing outward and was popularly called the *devatakotuva*.

The stupas originally had one umbrella placed symbolically over the relics enshrined. This number gradually increased with many stone *chatras* placed one above the other in a reducing cone shape. The enclosing process continued and the number not only increased further but these units of architecture also began to be built out of brick and mortar. Thus the brick masonry was able to indicate only the edge of each chatra unlike in the phase when stone was used with a central *yasti*. The brick *chatravali* is well plastered and the shadow lines of each *chatra* are seen in contrast against direct light. This feature ends up in the capping with a metal *kota* which is also designed as a series of *chatras* and a crystal placed at its peak.

The brilliant design of the architects of old was developed gradually, culminating in the great stupa of the Jetavana which stands even today as a towering monument to the masters of brick-masonry. The relics of such a stupa are enshrined at foundation-level, terrace-level and top-of-dome-level. The size of these chambers is determined by the length of the stone lintels that can be hewn, and so is relatively modest, despite the immensity of these edifices. Thus the Jetavana stupa, the tallest Buddhist monument in the world, is until today, from the point of view of brick technology, still the tallest edifice constructed of this material. Therefore, both from a religious and a technological point of view, the Jetavana stupa qualifies as an outstanding monument of mankind.

Other monuments

The ruins visible today above ground level belong to the last cultural phase of the site: the ninth to tenth centuries A.D. The gradual evolution of the whole monastery complex commenced at the northern end of the site in the latter half of the third century A.D., with the stupa as its focal

Image House, Jetavena, Anuradhapura, 8th-9th centuries.
This was probably a vaulted image house with a colossal Buddha figure in brick masonry and stucco. Only the pedestal and the giant stone reliquary is found today.

Plan of Image House, Jetavana
1. Entrances
2. Enclosed Mandapa
3. Circumambulation Path
4. Cells

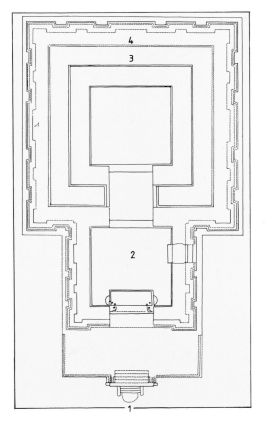

point, gradually spreading to the south and east over a period of about six centuries. While the earlier constructions were of brick, stone came into vogue as a building material ·during the later centuries, and even some of the older brick buildings were enlarged using this new material.

Next in order of importance to the Stupa are the *Bodhi* Tree and the Image House. At Jetavanaramaya, although no monument has been found to date which can be identified with certainty as a Bodhi Tree Shrine, the monastery can claim the largest Image House in Anuradhapura, as well as the largest twenty-five chamber stone reliquary so far discovered in Sri Lanka.

The large *patimaghara* or image house situated to the west of the stupa is a very impressive edifice with its eight-metre high monolithic door jambs, its twenty-four compartment stone reliquary and the lotus pedestal of the vanished Buddha image. The massive brick walls, pierced with tall, narrow windows, originally carried a brick-vaulted roof, parts of which have survived intact. The Buddha image would have been in brick and mortar, as evidence in the lotus pillar indicates.

Other important monuments so far identified include the residential quarter of the monks, the *Uposathagara*, or Confession Hall, an alms hall, several image houses, a large brick-built well in the form of a lotus leaf, a circular structure, and many ancient pathways. Historical literature and inscriptions refer to other types of buildings used for various purposes such as water pavilions, rooms to store the valuable gifts received by the monasteries.

The residential quarters are grouped in units of five, with the area enclosed by tall boundary walls, each with a main entrance and a secondary entrance. In a few examples, the main five-unit residential area within the boundary is separated by a brick wall from a group of subsidiary buildings. The purpose of these has not been satisfactorily established, but it is thought that they probably accommodated the lay officials and servants, since the large monasteries, being by far the biggest landowners in the country, needed an extensive lay establishment of officials and servants to administer their wordly affairs.

To the south of the Stupa, the remains of a large monument generally referred to as the 'Buddhist Railing Site' is a particularly interesting example of early Buddhist architecture. This rectangular structure, 43 by 34 metres in extent, has a stone railing consisting of seven horizontal members rising to a height of 1.6 metres. Its four entrances, one in the centre of each side, are orientated to the four cardinal points. Inside the enclosed area are the rows of columns which carried the superstructure. The area in which this monument stands has been in occupation from before the time of the foundation of the Jetavana monastery until the last days of the Anuradhapura Kingdom in the tenth or eleventh century.

This unique example of ancient Sinhalese architecture lies within a vast enclosed area bounded by brick boundary walls, more than one metre thick. Access to the sacred precinct is through an entrance porch in the centre of each side. The central edifice, as well as the whole of the enclosed area, has been enlarged at least twice, as archaeological data confirm. The

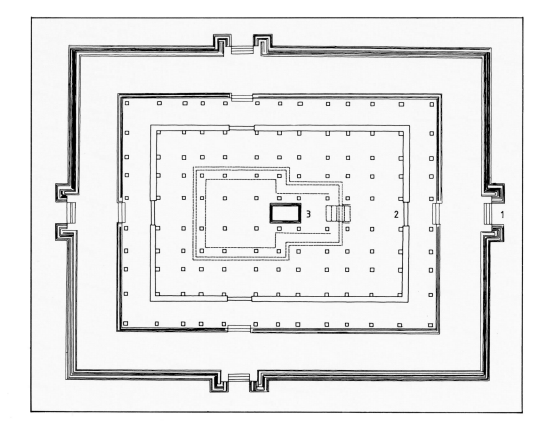

Plan, Bo-tree Court
1. Entrance
2. Covered Enclosure
3. Site of the Bo-tree

Stone parapet, Jetavana, Anuradhapura, 9th-10th centuries.
This vedi popularly called the "Buddhist Railing" is the stylised form of a post-and-horizontal fence design used from early times in association with Buddhist shrines.

principal monument is surrounded by the remains of other buildings, the purpose of which has yet to be identified.

Whether this building was an image house or a Bodhi Tree shrine is debatable at present. The most likely interpretation is that this was a special type of image house for a ceremony, referred to in the *Mahavamsa*, involving the ritual anointment of Buddha Images.

Some of the important building complexes, such as the *Uposathagara*, or Confession Hall and its sacred compound, have wide, high entrance porches. The Conference Hall of the Jetavana Monastery, situated to the south of the stupa, lies within a sacred enclosure measuring 115 by 86 metres, entered through a main entrance porch with steps at the sides. The main building, of brick construction, has a frontage of 34.5 metres and a maximum depth of 18.8 metres. Its smaller stone porch has to be entered from the south. The close spacing of its massive stone pillars indicate that this building was multi-storeyed. The superstructure would have been of timber, with a roof of copper tiles. Evidence from archaeological excavations indicates that the building was destroyed by fire. Of the many minor buildings of the complex, one has tentatively been identified as a water pavilion.

The two large pillared buildings with four entrances to the north and south of the *Uposathaghara* are thought to be preaching halls for the lay devotees who came to worship at the stupa. The devotees have to climb up to the high entrance porch, descend to the processional path, and mount to the level of the stupa by one of the flights of nineteen steps at each of the cardinal points. Around the processional path is a high wall connected to the porches and built of stone slabs, set vertically, on each face, the inside being filled with rammed earth, brickbats and rubble, and capped with coping stones.

The Jetavana treasure

The excavations in the Jetavana Monastery Complex have brought to light a great number of ruins, as well as artefacts, collectively known as the 'Jetavana Treasure'. The artefacts include imported ceramic ware, as well as locally manufactured vessels whose shapes, forms and functions are conceptually influenced by countries to the west, north and east of Sri Lanka; intaglio seals made of semi-precious stones and glass, with local and foreign subjects; Roman, Indian and other foreign coins; more than 300,000 beads fabricated from a wide range of materials - clay, glass, stone, precious and semi-precious stones, crystal, agate, carnelian, ivory, bone, shell, gold and silver, as well as bronze-ware and etched beads; pendants, tooth and bone amulets; shell, turned ivory, bronze and glass bangles; shell, ivory, bone, carnelian gold and bronze rings; a large collection of turned and carved ivories and bone seals; bronze ornaments; bronze hinges and nails; jewellery in a great variety of materials including lead; crystal reliquaries and reliquary spires; seven gold sheets containing assorted pages of the sacred Mahayana text Prajnaparamita inscribed on it; polished and unpolished precious stones; slabs of stone with paintings; sculptures carved out of both local and imported stone; Buddhist and Hindu bronzes and ritual objects, and imported raw materials such as carnelian and lapis lazuli.

With a few exceptions, most of these treasures were buried at the foot of the northern and eastern frontispieces, the *vahalkada* or *ayaka*, and under the upper stone-paved terrace of the Jetavana Stupa. The majority were unearthed during investigations to study the technologies employed in the construction of the colossal stupas of Anuradhapura. They were deposited in the thick clay layer between the basal platform and a brick upper platform built during the original construction of the stupa by Mahasena. Most of these artefacts can be dated on contextual and stylistic grounds to between the second century B.C., to the last quarter of the third century A.D.

The ivories, both turned and carved, numbering about 400 pieces in varying states of preservation, belong to about thirty categories of artefacts. Most important among these are the head of a *makara* carrying a garland. The spires of reliquaries illustrate very clearly the development of the stupa finial. A few bone seals, semi-hemispherical in shape, with a transverse hole close to the top, display the eight auspicious symbols. Some examples show vessels which have parallels with the Begram ivories, and can be attributed to the same period. Many ivory and bone dice, in different sizes with from one to four circles engraved on the four sides, were also found with a votive offering. Some were blanks, while a few had a circle at one end.

Makara and Human Head, Jetavana, Anuradhapura, 4th-5th centuries. A fine piece of carved marble found in excavations.

Prajnaparamita Sutta, Jetavana, Anuradhapura, 8th century.
The golden book of the Prajnaparamita Sutta was discoverd buried in the ground in a pot for safety. It is a text of Mahayana Buddhism which is worshipped as Dharmadhatu.

The use of ivory as a raw material in Sri Lanka goes back to the remote past. Both Pali and Sinhala literature carry references to ivory artefacts. The first direct reference to such an object in Sinhalese literature is found in the *Mahavamsa* in a description of the second-century B.C. Brazen Palace of King Dutthagamani Abhaya: 'Within the pavilion, gaily adorned with the seven gems, stood a shining beauteous throne of ivory with a seat of mountain crystal, and ivory back. On it were carved scenes from the *Jataka* tales.'

The *Culavamsa* refers to an ivory Chair of State carved with 'a beautiful, charming figure representing the *bodhisatta*, as beautiful as if it had been produced by a miraculous power', made by King Jettatissa II in the fourth Century A.D., at the request of his father, King Mahasena, the founder of Jetavanaramaya.

The ceramic group includes about 150 complete or near-complete vessels, some of which are imports from Western Asia and Northern India. One jar, with a spherical body, seems to have influenced the 'pot of plenty' motif carried in the hand of the guardian figures depicted in the characteristic Sri Lankan guardstones and at the base of the *kalpavrksa* or 'Tree of Life' representations. A number of glazed potsherds found in the earth-fill brought from an area outside the monument indicates that Partho-Sasanian wares were known in Sri Lanka for a considerable period of

Relief Sculpture of Mayadevi, Jetavana,
Anuradhapura, 4th-5th centuries.
A fine depiction of Mayadevi being guided to
the Sala Grove for the Birth of the Buddha.

time prior to the construction of the Jetavana stupa. The fine Red Polished Ware vessels, the later Red Polished Ware and the Red Slipped Pinkish-Buff Ware were also imported from India.

One particularly elaborate pitcher, incorporating the principles of hydrostatics, displays a creeper in relief on its shoulder and a transverse horizontal hole located halfway down its belly. Its handle has a tube-like cavity extending from the belly with an opening at the top. The clay used in the fabrication of this pitcher is almost identical to that used in local vessels discovered along with these moulded decorations. Clearly of local fabrication, it also shows foreign technological and ornamental influence in its construction and decoration: this pitcher can be assigned to a period before the end ot the third century A.D. A similar ceramic vessel with a grape-vine in relief on its shoulder can be seen among the Begram finds in Afghanistan.

A number of fragments of Rouletted Ware storage jars with black resin-lined interiors and terracotta handles, and many fragments of Islamic and Chinese ware have also been excavated at the Jetavana complex, in addition to other assorted wares which have not yet been identified. The fragments of glazed tile, stratigraphically assignable to a period prior to the last quarter of the third century A.D., are interesting in that they establish that glazed tiles were in use in Sri Lanka from that early period.

Of the sixteen intaglios or carved jewels, one is moulded in glass, while the majority are in carnelian, with a few in garnet. Thirteen of these, including one in the form of a plano-convex glass lens carved with the head of a male figure, have been found in association with the offerings deposited at the base of the stupa. Another identical lens was found along with it and is possibly its back support. A similar but broken flat glass lens shows part of a female figure with one leg pendant. Of the two carved carnelian seals, one depicts a Roman head, and the other shows a Roman figure. The rest, similar in shape and size, depict local animals and birds, and are of local origin. Carnelian blanks found at the Jetavana and elsewhere indicate that seal carving was practised in ancient Sri Lanka, using carnelian imported from abroad.

The more than 300,000 beads recovered are of different shapes, and in size they range from a medium-size mustard seed to about 4.5 cm in length. Some of the bronze beads are etched or gold-plated. This collection is an invaluable source of information on bead shapes and techniques of bead manufacture up to the last quarter of the third century A.D. It is also of immense importance for research on trade, cultural contacts and technology transfer. A large number of bangle fragments made of bronze, shell, ivory and glass have also been recovered. Some, of polychrome glass, were probably imports from the west. Materials used for rings include carnelian, gold, shell, ivory, bronze and bronze wire. Many are in the form of signet rings.

A large number of glass fragments were recovered from the excavations at the foot of the stupa. The majority are dark blue in colour, while two are purple with a whitish band. With the exception of these two pieces, the rest are rim, neck, body and base fragments and probably belong to goblets, bowls, or bottles. One complete bottle which has been recovered

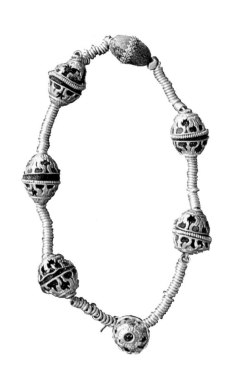

Gold Filigree Chain, Jetavana, Anuradhapura,
3rd-4th centuries.
A delicately designed chain with intricately
carved geometric designs.

is about five centimetres in height, with a thick body and a dark blue colour. Some vessels, partly reconstructed from fragments, indicate that they were originally hemispherical in shape. Two belong to mosaic vessels. Fragments of a few bases have also been found, one of which is convex in section. These are imports from Western Asia, either directly or through North-West India, and are attributable to the period before the last quarter of the third century A.D. It is possible that these small fragments of glass were considered precious, and were offered as gems in the enshrinements. Two fragments with a wavy decoration are of a type found in glass vessels discovered at Begram.

The bronze material includes decorative pieces, hooks, khol sticks, very small nails, and two small hinges. The hinges had been attached to an ivory chest, only the lid of which is preserved. The *svastika*-motifs attached to the ivory lid are of local origin. This is the same motif found in the pitcher with a handle referred to earlier. A few thin strips of bronze, about five millimetres wide, carry shallow carvings and must have been part of an ivory chest or similar object. A lion's leg in bronze, about four centimetres high, is part of a small stand or tripod and is of Western Asian or Roman origin.

Bronze artefacts from a much later period have also been found in the Jetavana excavations. A bronze stand in two parts is probably part of an object of a type used by Tibetan monks for meditation. It is of open work and carries on its body what appear to be Tantrayana deities. Of the eight Hindu bronzes, the Siva figure is the largest. The standing Bodhisatva figure belongs to an earlier period, around the sixth to seventh century A.D., than the bronze stand described above. It has been provided with a pedestal similar to that of the Hindu figures. Another figure has the inscription 'Nanadesin' inscribed on its pedestal in Pallava Grantha characters from the tenth to twelfth centuries A.D., and could be an import from Southern India. Two Pattini figures were found, one of which is of fine workmanship. In general, the Hindu bronzes can be ascribed to the eleventh to thirteenth centuries.

Among the most interesting sculptures discovered at Jetavana are two female figures in the round, larger than life-size and carved out of dolomite; one of them, which has conserved its head, has a *padma*, or lotus headdress. What appears to be Amarvati marble was used for several of the small fragments of sculpture in the round, as well as a particularly interesting relief sculpture of three female figures. The single, unfinished guardstone, carved with a guardian deity, datable to the ninth century, is probably the finest of its type discovered to date, and is a veritable store-house of information on the different types of stone-carving.

Of the painted slabs identified as belonging to the *ayakas*, or frontispieces, of the stupa, one which has been cleaned and conserved shows a line of geese on its upper edge, while the underneath bears traces of lapis lazuli. They can be attributed to the third century A.D., to the reign of King Mahasena, who built this feature of the stupa.

Among the most spectacular of the discoveries, and that which has attracted international attention, is what is known as the Jetavana Gold Plates. Discovered among potsherds by two labourers during excavations

Crystal Reliquary, Jetavana, Anuradhapura, 5th-6th centuries.
The holy relics of the Buddha or of an Arhat were normally placed in such a relic casket. The stopper, designed as the superstructure of a stupa, was used to cover the container.

in the south-west quadrant in 1982, this is an incomplete set of gold plates, each measuring approximately 63 by 7.5 centimetres and inscribed with fragments of a Mahayana text identified as the *Prajnaparamita Sutra*, a philosophical discourse of the Buddha with his disciples, written in Sanskrit language in a ninth-century Sinhala script containing some archaic letter forms.

Other gold objects of particularly fine workmanship include a tiny jug with a handle made of very thin sheet gold, a fragment depicting fourteen four-petalled flowers, a gold necklace with barrel-shaped beads in open-work repoussée technique, and gold-plated beads from excavations at the foot of the stupa, showing that the technique of gold plating was known and practised in Sri Lanka as early as the third century A.D.

Polonnaruva

The medieval capital

P. L. Prematilleke and L. K. Karunaratne

Polonnaruva, the medieval capital of Sri Lanka from the eleventh to the end of the first quarter of the thirteenth century A.D., is situated in the Dry Zone of the North-Central province. Archaeological evidence for the early habitation in Polonnaruva goes back to the second century B.C. A study the nearby of primeval forests of Habarana (land of Sabaras or prehistoric tribes) would enable the history of human occupation of Polonnaruva and the suburbs to be traced back to remote times.

During the first millennium A.D., when Sri Lanka's capital, Anuradhapura, was flourishing, Polonnaruva served as a fortified outpost (*kandavuru-nuvara*) where Sinhala garrisons camped during periods of internal strife between the rivals of Anuradhapura in the north and Mahagama in the south. The strategic significance of Polonnaruva lay in its ability to command the river crossings of the Mahaveli, thus providing a buffer against the invading armies. Thus, Polonnaruva gained the status of an important city, even in Anuradhapura times.

The ancient Sinhala rulers built vast irrigation reservoirs almost from the beginning of written history, and by the twelfth century a flourishing agrarian economy had made Sri Lanka self-sufficient in food. The rulers of Anuradhapura, as recorded in the chronicles, constructed large reservoirs throughout the island. In the fourth century A.D., the great builder of reservoirs, King Mahasena, was responsible for the construction of the Minneriya (Manihira vapi) not far from Polonnaruva. The other reservoirs in and around Polonnaruva such as Giritale, Kaudulla and Topavava, are also the result of the irrigation activities of the Anuradhapura Kings. The Topavava, built in the sixth century by Upatissa II, and two other reservoirs were combined by the greatest ruler of Polonnaruva, Parakramabahu I, to form the Parakrama Samudra, or 'Sea of Parakrama'.

With the development of irrigation works and agricultural activities, Polonnaruva became a flourishing city. From about the seventh century, Polonnaruva became the country residence of the royalty of Anuradhapura. Being far from the north-western shores, which acted as an entry-point for the South-Indian invader, and also being on the ancient highway, Polonnaruva enjoyed a highly strategic position, and gradually became as important as the thousand-year-old city of Anuradhapura.

Sri Lanka was involved in Indian politics by the tenth century, when Sri Lanka sent forces to the Pandyans, its allies in the wars against the Colas. The Colas, however, proved too powerful for the alliance, and this

King or Sage? Pothgulvehera, Polonnaruva, 12th century.
Popularly called Prakramabahu I.

Alahana Parivena, Polonnaruva, 12th century.
Crematory Stupas, Lankatilaka and Kirivehera.
(overleaf)

endangered Sri Lanka's political situation. After a series of repeated attacks, the Cola ruler Rajaraja I was finally able to conquer Anuradhapura and devastate the city, leading to its final abandonment. The Colas established their rule in Polonnaruva through a viceroy, instituting an almost military administration in the capital, and Polonnaruva was renamed 'Jananatha-mangalam' after the Cola ruler. During their occupation, which lasted nearly eight decades, Hindu religious ideals, particularly Saivism, were fostered. This is seen in the large number of ruins of Hindu monuments that exist in the ancient city.

The Sinhala kingship was re-established in 1055 under Vijayabahu I (1055-1110) who was able to bring about a renaissance of Sinhala Buddhist cultural activities. Vijayabahu I was the first ruler to establish Polonnaruva as the capital, although several kings of Anuradhapura had resided in Polonnaruva temporarily, during the latter half of the period. Vijayabahu himself had his coronation ceremony held in Anuradhapura. During this period Buddhism had declined and ordained monks had to be brought from Burma. Monastic edifices were restored, and the shrine, known as Atadage, which housed the sacred tooth relic and the bowl relic, is attributed to this period.

Vijayabahu's peaceful reign was followed by a period of internecine wars between heirs to the throne. However, after about four decades, the great ruler Parakramabahu I (1153 -1186) emerged to commence yet another golden era for Sri Lanka. It is this versatile king who was responsible for the construction of the Sea of Parakrama. Agricultural development reached its highest peak during his reign, and Sri Lanka became the 'Granary of the East'. The powerful ruler even invaded Burma in order to combat the reactionary activities of the Burmese ruler, Alaungsuthu, and was further able to display his might by invading the South-Indian Kingdom of Pandya.

Parakramabahu's liberal patronage of the arts excelled that of earlier rulers. He established great Buddhist monasteries such as the Alahana Parivena, the Veluvana Vihara, the Jetavana Vihara, the Uttararama, the Dakkhinarama and the Pacchimarama, lofty image shrines such as the Lankatilaka and the Tivamka-patimaghara, the rock-cut images of the Galvihara (ancient Uttararama), the Damilathupa and the Palace complex. The rock inscription at Galvihara records the unification of the divided monks by King Parakramabahu. Nissankamalla followed the foot-steps of Parakramabahu and embellished the city with a large amount of varied monuments, the vestiges of which exhibit even today the grandeur that was Polonnaruva.

Planning and layout

The city of Polonnaruva covers an area of about 122 hectares, spread out to a distance of five kilometres from north to south and three kilometres from east to west. Within this area are several groups of carefully planned building complexes, some fully and others partially excavated and conserved. The main city comprises a walled inner citadel and an outer walled city provided with four main gateways. The ancient gates to the east and west of the wide boundary wall enclosing the present city have been unearthed during recent excavations of its northern, eastern and western sectors. The wall had apparently been built at two different stages;

the lower part, built earlier, appears to be well-preserved, and has even retained its original plasterwork in situ.

The streets are laid out on a regular grid, orientated north-south and east-west. The walled citadel, containing the royal palace complex, covers an area of ten acres. The buildings within the citadel and those outside it conform to their individual requirements and are carefully planned on terraces. The architects have taken advantage of the undulations of the site to set out terraces, avenues and pathways at different levels. The building complexes were also surrounded by forest reserves and parks. Water, an essential requirement in the dry zone, was provided by building large reservoirs and an extensive network of tanks and channels. The great man-made lake Parakrama Samudra, 2,500 hectares in extent, has a capacity of 134 million cubic metres.

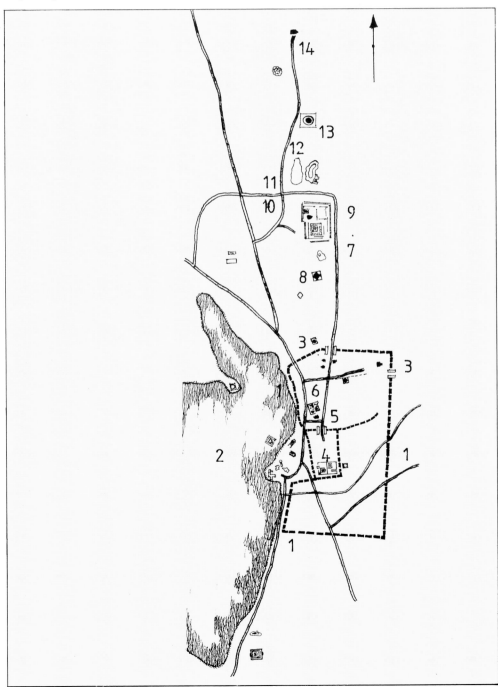

Ancient city of Polonnaruva
1. *Outer city walls*
2. *Man-made Reservoirs*
3. *Outer city gates*
4. *Inner city*
5. *Inner city gates*
6. *Tooth Relic Complex*
7. *Alahana Parivena*
8. *Rankoth Vehera*
9. *Baddasimapasada*
10. *Lankatilaka*
11. *Kirivehera*
12. *Galvihara*
13. *Damilathupa*
14. *Tivamkapilimage*

The architecture of Polonnaruva is a continuation of the early Anuradhapura building tradition. The Polonnaruva rulers attempted to create a new ideal, yet following the older models. This is evident in the numerous building types that evolved between the eleventh and twelfth centuries. Although the South Indian occupation did exert some influence over the indigenous style, as is seen particularly in the *vimana-panjara-kudu* style ornamentation of the exterior walls of the image houses, the building of the Hindu shrines did not influence the style of the Sri Lankan architects to a significant extent. The existence of several suburban monasteries around the city of Polonnaruva bears witness to the prosperity of the area long before the city itself came to be built. It is, however, in the twelfth-century sites that the best examples of Polonnaruva architecture is to be found.

The Buddhist monasteries of Polonnaruva provide the best surviving examples of image shrines, stupas, chapter houses, hospitals and ponds. Three colossal brick-built shrines: the Thuparama, Lankatilaka and Tivamka-patimaghara, throw much light on the vaulted viharas (gedige) type described in commentaries from the thirteenth century. The stupas of Manikvehera, Rankotvehera, Kirivehera, Damilathupa and Satmahal-prasada are particularly significant, and of considerable interest in the study of the evolution of stupa design.

Another of the most striking features of Polonnaruva is the colossal scale of the sculptured images, particularly those representing the Buddha. The two brick images of Lankatilaka and Tivamka-patimaghara and the Galvihara group are notable among such gigantic sculptures. Many other sculptures of divinities, dancers and dwarfs testify to the degree of excellence attained by the Polonnaruva artists.

The principal groups of monuments making up the city of Polonnaruva, as we see it today, are described by and large in the order that they would be seen by a visitor starting from the southern entrance to the site and progressing to the north.

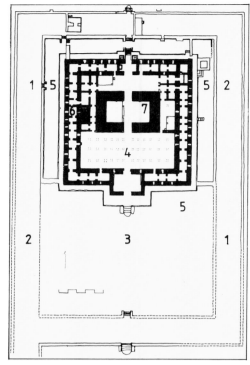

Palace of King Prakramabahu I
1. *Outer wall*
2. *Ground floor service rooms*
3. *Palace court*
4. *Audience Hall*
5. *Peripheral Guard Rooms*
6. *Stone Stairway*
7. *Inner Keep*

Potgul Vehera monastery

At the southern end of the city, outside the Royal Garden of Nandana Uyana is the monastery referred to as the Potgul Vehera, or the 'Library Monastery'. Its buildings are grouped on terraces around a central square terrace containing the principal monument, a circular shrine or library for sacred books. At the northern boundary of the site is a sculptured figure carved into the face of the rock outcrop. This figure has been a subject of study and conjecture by many scholars, who have interpreted it variously as the likeness of a king or a sage. The location of the site and the statue on the bund of the lake makes one wonder if it is a likeness of the great tank-builder and builder of the lake, King Parakramabahu himself. It could also very well be a representation of the sage Pulasti, after whom Polonnaruva was named Pulastipura.

The citadel and palace complex

Moving north from Potgul Vehera, we come to the Citadel with its storeyed palace complex, assembly hall, and the stone bathing pool of the royal

Palace of King Parakramabahu I, Polonnaruva,
12th century.
The brick masonry extends to the third floor.

garden. The smaller citadel of Nissankamalla, who succeeded Parakramabahu, is also in this area, situated in the ancient Dipuyyana.

The palaces of Parakramabahu and Nissankamalla, with their audience halls and the bathing ponds, provide an insight into the royal palace architecture of ancient Lanka. That of Parakramabahu is described in enthusiastic detail and probably much exaggeration in the Culavamsa. Accordingly, the palace is said to have had a thousand rooms, with hundreds of pillars of varying shapes, a dancing hall and banqueting hall and many other adjuncts.

In its general layout, ample galleries delimit a vast central courtyard containing, to the west, the main palace building, with its massive weathered brick walls pierced for beam-ends, which have been conserved up to a height of two storeys with fragments of the original stucco intact, enclosing small peripheral rooms surrounding the interior halls in much the same way that the outer galleries surround the palace building. Many smaller ancillary buildings of the same plan form can be seen to the south and east of the palace complex. The wooden superstructure of the upper floors has disappeared long ago, but fragments of a stone staircase can still be seen to the south; according to the chronicle, the palace counted seven storeys. Richly decorated windows would once have conferred on this grandiose ruin a sumptuous richness.

Council chamber of King Parkramabahu I, Polonnaruva, 12th century.
The stone pillars once supported a wide timber roof.

The audience hall of Parakramabahu, situated a little to the west of the palace, displays a classic example of an ancient royal council chamber, while that of Nissankamalla, has as a unique feature in the inscriptions on the pillars indicating the seats allocated to each minister, and the Lion Throne of Nissankamalla, on which the king sat.

The quadrangle

Leaving the citadel by its northern gate, one comes to the sacred quadrangle containing some of the earliest and most sacred monuments of Polonnaruva. The central unit here is the Vatadage, or circular relic house, which fulfills the role usually occupied by a stupa in the monastic complex of Dalada Maluva. Oriented towards the north, the Vatadage is entered via a strongly projecting porch giving access to a broad, raised circular terrace. Four flights of steps, preceded by moonstones of exceptional beauty, lead from this terrace by four entrance doors, now in ruins, oriented to the cardinal points, each of which has a seated Buddha image placed in its axis, into the shrine room. In its centre stood the dagaba, the object of veneration. Five concentric rows of columns, three on the outside and two on the inside, supported the heavy wooden roof structure, now disappeared. The balustrades flanking the entrances, the moonstones and other surviving architectural details, are of exceptional quality. The Circular Caitya Shrine (Vatadage) with its ornate design and decoration, represents the ultimate development of this type of religious architecture.

In the same quadrangle are many other buildings, all image houses. The Thuparama, a brick-built, vaulted shrine, which has come down to us in an almost perfect state of conservation, is also the oldest image house at Polonnaruva; although mentioned among the list of buildings erected by Parakramabahu I, it seems to be more ancient, and is ascribed by most scholars to the reign of Vijayabahu I (1055-1110).

The Nissankalatamandapa is a unique structure, having an unusual pillar type simulating a lotus stalk with the flower as the capital. Its outer walls

Vatadage or Circular Stupa House,
Polonnaruva, 12th century.
The stone pillars once supported a conical
timber roof.

take the form of a wooden railing assembled with mortice and tennon joints, imitated in stone. An inscription attributes this charming edifice to Nissankamalla, and relates how the king used to listen to recitals of the Buddhist scriptures there. The area also contains a Bo-Tree shrine, the Atadage and Hatadage relic shrines, the Satmahalprasada, a stupa of unusual stepped pyramidal form, and the Galpota, or 'Stone Book', an inscription recording the foundation and embellishment of the city.

Outside the terrace are the isolated ruins of a Hindu shrine, a relic of the Cola occupation. Further towards the eastern and southern gateways and isolated from the Buddhist shrines, stand the ruins of other Hindu temples, further reminders of the Cola occupation.

Manikvehera monastery complex

Leaving the outer city, one comes to the monastery complexes which comprise several stupas, shrine rooms and assembly halls as their central and dominant features.

The Manikvihara monastery complex, situated immediately north of the northern boundary wall of the ancient city, has revealed several significant features. The sacred terrace with the stupa, image house and Bodhi tree shrine, was constructed in at least two stages. The first stage appears to date from about the eighth century A.D. The stupa of Manikvehera is a

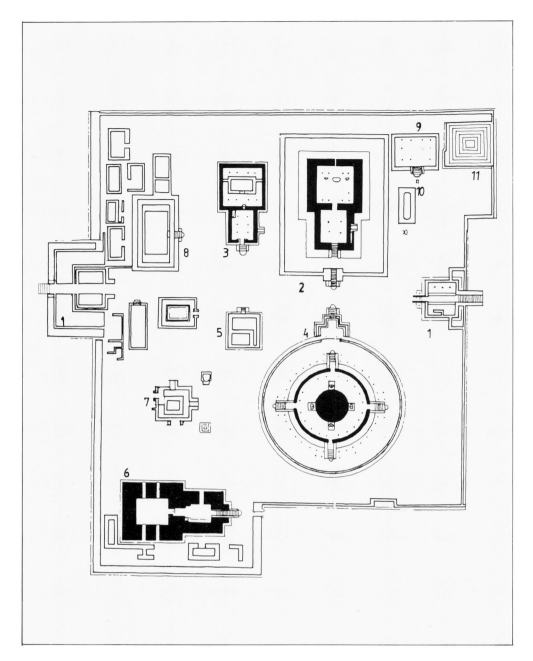

rare design built on a high walled terrace with a small lotus-shaped stupa in the centre. The image house with crystalline limestone images of the Buddha compares well with that of the eighth-century edifice at Medirigiriya.

The complex to the north of the sacred terrace appears to be a typical medical centre with cells arranged around the boundary and a large monk's cell in the centre of the courtyard. One pair of surgical forceps was unearthed from this site. Yet another vihara court to the north-east laid out by the pilgrims' path has revealed an interesting eighth-century Bodhi Tree shrine and a shrine on pillars, or *tampita vihara*, perhaps of a later date.

Alahana Parivena

To the north of the city, Parakramabahu I erected the vast complex known as Alahana Parivena, a monastic university which is now being fully excavated and landscaped. This important site, extending over an area of

Tooth Relic Shrine of Nissankamalla, Polonnaruva, 12th century.
A standing Buddha statue on the ground floor is seen in the distance. The Tooth Relic was enshrined on the upper floor.

more than eighty hectares, was selected for excavation and conservation under the UNESCO-Sri Lanka Cultural Triangle programme. Prior to commencement only about ten per cent of the area to the east of the sacred edifices had been excavated by the Archaeological Survey, under the direction of Senerath Paranavitana. Early archaeologists H.C.P. Bell and A.M. Hocart had done the pioneering work of clearing the monuments of the central terrace: the Kiri Vehera, Lankatilaka, and Baddhasimapasada.

The surrounding lower area, especially on the west side, had been filled with debris, almost covering the whole of the western terraces. Almost the whole monastery complex was covered with shrubs and trees and left to desolation. Over the last twelve years, excavations have unearthed a variety of structures and artefacts that provide a wealth of information for the reconstruction of the history of the Alahana Parivena monastery in particular and that of Polonnaruva in general, and recent discoveries include some of the most unique and significant buildings of the Polonnaruva period.

The monastery itself consisted of many separate units demarcated by smaller boundary walls with small entrance doorways. Each unit had its own living-cells, and several of them seem to have shared a common bath-house, refectory and other facilities. Excavations have exposed a large number of monks' cells, laid out according to a regular plan and apparently two-storeyed with tiled roofs. The structures are of simple plan with walls of mud reinforced with roughly hewn pillars erected on a brick platform.

At the heart of the site, a roughly square sacred enclosure contains several important groups of ruins and water-tanks. The brick-built image house of Lankatilaka, with its colossal standing Buddha statue, also of brick, occupies the centre of this space. This largest and most imposing sanctuary of Polonnaruva was rebuilt by Parakramabahu on the site of an earlier temple. The entrance facade, to the south, is the best-conserved, and gives an idea of the height to which its walls once rose. The exterior walls are articulated by four fictitious storeys separated by strongly moulded

Stucco relief sculpture at Lankatilaka, Polonnaruva, 12th century.
These reliefs display the architectural form of the brick vaulted buildings of the 12th century.

Lankatilaka Image-house, Polonnaruva, 12 century.
This was originally a brick vaulted structure with a stucco covered exterior.

cornices and divided by pilasters into decorative panels ornamented by representations of pavilions, all delicately sculpted in brick with a fine coating of stucco.

To the south-east of the Lankatilaka, is the Baddhasimapasada which is perhaps the largest chapter house in ancient Lanka and has all the amenities required for rehearsing the code of discipline by the monks. Twice every month, at the time of the new moon and the full moon, all the monks of the Alahana Parivena had to gather around their Abbot and make a public confession of their faults. Situated on a raised terrace reached by steps with moonstones, especially that to the west, of exceptional beauty, the central hypostyle hall or *poyage*, with its finely moulded columns, is surrounded by monks' cells grouped around a quadrangle with windows overlooking the surrounding landscape. The square central building appears, from the thickness of its outer walls, originally to have had upper floors,

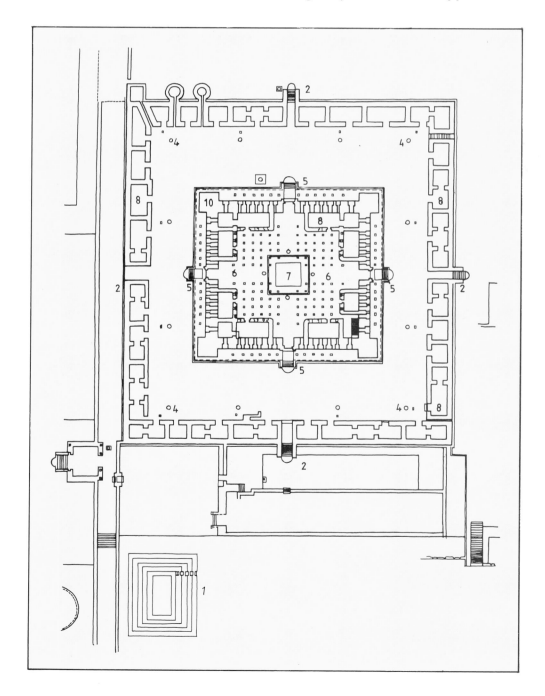

Baddasimapasada or Chapter House
1. *Cistern*
2. *Entrance*
3. *Cells of monks*
4. *Boundary stones*
5. *Entrance to the hall*
6. *Hall of the Chapter*
7. *Platform for senior monks*
8. *Cells of monks*
9. *Stone stairway*
10. *Heavy brick masonry*

Baddasimapasada or Chapter House,
Polonnaruva, 12th century.
The ground floor of this storeyed edifice was
used for the assembly of monks while the cells
in the storeys above were monastic residences.

and this is confirmed by the chronicle accounts of central assembly halls with up to twelve stories. The beautifully carved *purnaghata* pillars placed around the exterior of the edifice signify that the chapter house was meant only for ecclesiastical activities.

Kirivehera, perhaps erected by Queen Subhadra (Bhaddavati), one of the wives of Parakramabahu, is remarkable for the perfection of its proportions and is one of the best-conserved stupas in Sri Lanka; although restored several times, it appears to have retained its initial form. Many mounds which were originally minor stupas containing the corporeal remains of the royal family and the prelates of the monastery have been excavated. Excavation of the large mound to the east of the Kirivehera revealed a three-chambered relic block, which throws light on the types of relic chamber, built in the stupas. The double stupa to the south of the Lankatilaka image house could be an interesting edifice where two funerary stupas, perhaps of a king and queen, were built together.

A small chapter-house, or assembly hall for monks, located on the lower terrace to the west of Kirivehera, bears indications of a now-vanished upper storey. Two sets of boundary stones were placed at the four corners and the stairway has a unique square moonstone. Behind, a combined bath and toilet unit with separate pits, exemplifies the standard of sanitary facilities achieved at the time.

The Monks' Hospital discovered at Alahana Parivena is the first of its kind to be unearthed from Polonnaruva. The plan of the edifice resembles that at Mihintale, yet with some significant differences, having sanitary facilities attached to the living quarters and a separate treatment area. Artefacts found during excavations included medical equipment: a stone medicine trough or *behet-oruva*, a micro-balance, a spoon, herbal grinding stones, and storage jars of chinese celedon. Surgical instruments such as probes, forceps, scissors, scalpels and lancets are unique finds. These medical and surgical artefacts are important for the study of the hospital and health care systems of ancient Lanka.

The lotus ponds and stepped ponds are examples of the Polonnaruva architects' attempt to compensate for the grand designs of Anuradhapura by aesthetic diversity. Two of the square ponds which have been excavated and conserved are interesting appendages to the monastery complex. One of them, stepped in section and very deep, appears to have some resemblance to the stone-built pond in Hampi (Karnataka, India). These ponds probably served as storage tanks for water.

Rankot Vehera is a large stupa built in the tradition of the Mahavihara stupas of early Anuradhapura. This stupa was partially conserved prior to work being undertaken in 1981 by the Cultural Triangle, and has now been fully conserved and its terrace set out. The stupa rests on a square paved platform surrounded by a wide sand path and provided with entrances at the cardinal points, with roadways leading to them. The stupa superstructure was built with a brick core, the space between the core and the outer dome cover being filled with earth.

Kirivehera or Milk Stupa, Polonnaruva, 12th century.
The heavily-plastered brick stupa was originally painted in many layers of shining white lime wash.

*Rankot Vehera or the Gold Pinacled Stupa,
Polonnaruva, 12th century.
A brick edifice of colossal proportions in the
Alahana Parivena.*

Artefacts and inscriptions

A significant aspect of the systematic excavations carried out at Alahana
Parivena has been the retrieval of small and large artefacts relating to the
monuments and the history of the site. Thus, the written history can now
be confirmed and clarified by inscriptional data and artefacts. Pottery forms
the largest collection as sherds and whole pots. Pottery excavated from
Alahana Parivena Project include begging bowls, plates, cooking vessels
and jas, lids, as well as lamps, underground pipes and even ovens. These
show the continuity of the earlier types of Anuradhapura, yet their quality
appears to have declined. Bricks were found in hundreds of different shapes
to suit their use and are of high quality.

All of the foreign ceramics discovered at this site are Chinese Sung
period ware, including 'Timokku' tea bowls specially made for the royal
family. Many bronze coins were found, and the bronze statues of Hindu
gods discovered at Kali Kovil are among the best products of the age,
displaying considerable skill in bronze-casting. The large number of crucibles
discovered throws light on the extent of the metal-casting industry of the
period, and the production of jewellery and other ornamental objects. A
large bronze jewellery casket discovered at Alahana Parivena is a unique
find which could possibly be of foreign origin, and a bronze gilt chalice,
similar to Chinese drinking cups of ancient times, is yet another rare and
important find. Glassware, including bangles, beads and seals, also provide
useful data for the study of the social history of medieval times.

The skeletal remains of a twelfth or thirteenth century man discovered
during excavation at Alahana Parivena are among the very rare remains of
historic man to be found in Sri Lanka. The most recent discoveries from

*Teracotta lamp, Polonnaruva, 12th century.
Many teracotta objects have been found in the
excavations.*

the moat of the ancient city of the skeletons of what may have been two soldiers together with swords and other weapons, provide unique data for the study of the past.

Other activities of the Project include documenting the inscriptions of Polonnaruva. In the course of this study, several new records of historical importance were discovered. One such record is that of a boundary stone mentioning the southern limit of the crematory ground on which the Alahana Parivena was subsequently built and named 'the Crematory Monastery'. Another record on a pillar refers to a monk of the Dharmaruci order, the powerful Mahayana sect that prevailed during the eighth to tenth centuries in Anuradhapura and elsewhere. Two identical inscriptions by Nissankamalla, record a request to the monks to use their avocation for the benefit of the people and the religion by limiting their activities to *Ganthadhura* (literary work) and *Vipassanadhura* (meditation).

Galvihara

To the north of Alahana Parivena, Pakramabahu I founded another great religious complex known as the 'Northern Monastery' or Uttararama, in the chronicle. Galvihara, the most celebrated site in Polonnaruva and one of the most famous on the whole island, is known, for its large rock-cut images which are in a perfect state of preservation. From left to right, the group consists of a great sitting Buddha, an artificial cavern cut out of the rock, and an upright and a reclining Buddha. The standing image, its hands placed across the chest, probably portrays the second week after

Samadhi Image at Galvihara, Polonnaruva, 12th century.
This statue is one of the masterpieces of Sri Lankan Buddhist sculpture.

Galvihara or Rock Monastery, Polonnaruva, 12th century.
This retains some of the finest collections of Buddhist sculpture found anywhere in the world.

Enlightenment. These figures give an idea of other colossal statues of the same period such as the Great Buddha of the Lankatilaka which were executed in perishable materials and have vanished without trace. The modern name of the site, 'Galvihara', refers to this sculptured rock-face.

Excavations here have unearthed an ancient refectory for monks. The site of the rock-cut images at Galvihara has also been investigated to find the plan of the structures. The central terrace may have been a *mandapa* built as an assembly hall where the congregation of monks was held by the king for the purpose of uniting the divided sangha. Each image, different in posture and size, seems to have been contained in a separately covered shrine. The difference in height and size of each would certainly have given the whole complex a very interesting façade which may well have been largely of brick and timber, although unfortunately no trace of it remains. However, the elaborate carving of buildings with a decorative gateway seen in the background of the seated image gives an idea of the building of the shrines. These closely resemble the façades of the brick-built structures at Lankatilaka and Tivamka Pilimage and might in the case of Galvihara have been of wood and plaster.

The Northern temple

Situated at the northernmost boundary of the ancient city is the large monastery complex believed to be the ancient Jetavanarama or the Veluvanarama. The image house, or Tivamka-patimaghara, enjoys fame for several reasons.

A vaulted brick-built image house similar to the Thuparama and the Lankatilaka, it was built to house one of the tallest standing brick-built images of the Buddha in the Tivamka posture, displaying a uniquely relaxed stance.

This shrine also contains a unique collection of twelfth-century murals of the classical school of painting, a continuation of the earlier periods seen at Sigiriya and Ajanta. Polonnaruva continued the earlier painting tradition on a larger scale for both secular and religious edifices, where the medium of *fresco secco* was used universally, for decoration as well as edification. The Tivamka-patimaghara is outstanding among the religious shrines in preserving most of its paintings, and constitutes the only pictorial group from Polonnaruva to have survived to the present day. Those on the outer walls are purely decorative, while the wall-paintings of the interior

Lotus Pond, Polonnaruva, 12th century. The ornamented bath is one of a few in the park to the north of the Alahana Parivena.

106

A Worshipping figure in stucco, Polonnaruva, 12th century.

depict the past births of the Buddha (*jataka*) and his life incidents. These murals display the stylistic evolution of the early classical paintings of Ajanta and Sigiriya, and come closer to the post-classical regional styles of Sittannavasal and Panamalai in South India.

In the monastery garden of the Northern Temple is a bath built of stone in the shape of an open lotus. Many more such baths of lotus design built in the monastery grounds, probably to contain water for the use of the monks, lie in ruins and are yet to be excavated and conserved.

Damilathupa, perhaps the largest stupa built in Polonnaruva, being over 200 metres in diameter at the base, seems not to have reached the height to which it was originally intended to rise. Excavation revealed that the stupa had been built by enclosing an existing quartzite hill. The structure of the base has revealed a ring type construction, and a stabilized gravel

Bodhisattva figure, Tivanka Pilimage, Polonnaruva, 12th century.
A classical composition of a group of deities.

fill to the interior to fill the area up to the limit of the natural mound. Investigations are continuing in order to find data to determine the form of the stupa, which is scheduled to be conserved accordingly. When fully cleared, it will certainly be most imposing, and perhaps the largest stupa of the Northern temple complex in Polonnaruva.

The Hindu temples

Polonnaruva has perhaps the largest number of Hindu temples spread out amidst the Buddhist shrines and located within the ancient city limits, almost on the periphery of the Alahana Parivana complex. They thus form part of the extended layout of the ancient sites in and around this area. It is intended to be part and parcel of the major work of the conservation of monuments in Polonnaruva undertaken by the UNESCO-Sri Lanka Cultural Triangle Project, and their excavation and conservation will add greatly to our understanding of the civilization of the island and of the Polonnaruva period.

Compared to the larger Buddhist shrines of the Vatadage or Jetavanarama, the Hindu temples can be considered small but significant in design and execution, with a definite Hindu character conforming to an orthodox religious architectural tradition, and it is clear that these temples are the work of architects conversant with the practice of Hindu temple architecture. Whilst most have been built entirely in stone, a few have stone plinths and a brick superstructure; a method also not uncommon in the building of Buddhist temples in Polonnaruva. Only the Siva Devales of Polonnaruva have a totally stone-built form.

The discovery in 1975 of several large images of Hindu Gods buried at the site of the Naipena Vihara, a Hindu shrine, explains how in later years a Hindu shrine came to be identified as a Buddhist temple. The reason for the burial of these images is not known. They were in an excellent state of conservation when discovered and are now in the Anuradhapura Museum. Indian iconographers who have examined the bronzes have expressed the opinion that they may have been executed by local craftsmen.

Within the Alahana Parivena complex itself several Hindu shrines have been constructed. One of structures recently excavated contained two significant stone sculptures of Surya and Parasurama, now in the Colombo Museum. Another significant recent discovery was the identification of an earlier bronze of Parvati, now in Colombo museum, as the missing one from the pedestal of a Siva-Parvati combination, of which only the Siva statue was in position when the archaeologists found it.

The location of Hindu shrines in Polonnaruva is interesting, and can be a useful index to the observance of Hindu ritual by Buddhists in a strictly Buddhist atmosphere. Starting with the southern and between the Potgulvehera and the Nissanka Maligava there are the ruins of two small Hindu temples on the bund of Parakrama Samudra.

Siva Devale 1, a large stone-built Hindu shrine near the quadrangle located below the terrace, commands an important position almost at the entrance to the citadel. The next largest Hindu shrine is the well-preserved stone building near the Pabaluvehera complex known as Siva Devale No.2.

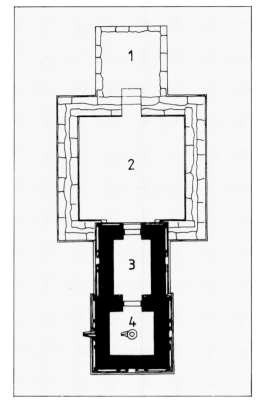

Sivalinga Shrine No. 1.
1. Entrance Porch
2. Open Mandapa
3. Ambulatory
4. Cells

God Siva, Polonnaruva, 12th century.
A product of the period of the Chola
occupation of Sri Lanka.

Goddess Parvati, Polonnaruva, 12th century.
The consort of God Siva.

A Hindu complex is seen on either side of the south gate, while outside the gate is a Buddhist monastery.

The cultural Triangle excavations at the Kali–Kovil also unearthed six bronze statues of Siva–Candrasekara, Parvati, and a Siva–bhakta of excellent workmanship. Immediately outside, a large complex of shrines appears lining an ancient street. This area may have been totally occupied by a population of Hindus who perhaps held high position in the government, or were an immigrant trading population.

The Shrines located close to the edge of the lake are devoted to various deities. The images discovered, some of stone and others of bronze, are now in the museum. The sculptures of the attributes carried in the hands of the Gods is clear and of the same degree of excellence as seen in the images of Galvihara.

The shrine referred to as Naipena Vihara is interesting in that it is totally brick-built and very much in the form of a Buddhist shrine. It is here that the largest collection of bronzes was found. What is interesting is how this Hindu Shrine came to be known in later years as Naipena Vihara. This wrong identification was due to the cobra-hood decorations of the *stupika* of the shrine, now fallen down. In front of this are the ruins of a connected temple structure including a small shrine built entirely in stone.

Beyond this site on the same street is a large site bounded by a peripheral wall. This has all the features of a Hindu Shrine including a holy well, and individual shrines devoted to Ganesha, Vishnu, the Nandi Mandapam etc., all spaciously laid out. Much still remains to be discovered in this area.

In later years the diminishing cultivator population set up small shrines to local deities following the ritual as practised at a Hindu Temple.

The inscription at the Preeti–Dana–Mandapaya, the alms hall of Nissankamalla. is of particular interest. It speaks of the existence of an orchard in and around the Hindu shrines from which the public were forbidden to gather fruit. This orchard probably supplied the Hindu temples with the requirements for their daily pooja and as can be expected it was maintained by land allocated to the temple for its exclusive use.

The street leads one to the Northern temple and beyond to the colony and ancient sites of Hatamune, Minneriya and Madirigiriya.

There is a clear geographical separation of the Hindu temples from the Buddhist shrines, and their location suggests exclusive use by royalty of the area around the Hatadage and city limits. Those on the old roadway to the North formed the temples for the use of a resident or immigrant population, and probably of traders or government employees, as well as relations of the queens during their frequent visits to the island.

The excavation and conservation of these monuments has yielded valuable material leading to an understanding of the Hindu shrines and their identity in the Polonnaruva period. The discovery of these sites and their clearing was done as early as 1890. During this work it is creditable that not only were the sites carefully located and inventorized, but also thorough records and detailed survey drawings were made recording the architectural plan forms and details. These early records have become invaluable sources of information in the work of conservation.

'The Saiva bronzes of Polonnaruva are in all respects very different from the old Buddhist works. They may have been cast in Ceylon, but as a group they belong to the prolific South-Indian school of medieval bronzes represented by the Madras Natrajas and the Tanjors Siva. The subjects include Siva and Parvati, with Nandi, images of the Saiva saints, the Sun-god, and one or two figures of Krishna. They probably mark one of the periods of Tamil occupation of Polonnaruva, though the possibility is by no means excluded that Siva Devales flourished contemporaneously with the Buddhist viharas without conflict.' (A.K. Coomaraswamy, 'Bronzes in the Colombo Museum').

The gardens of Polonnaruva

Polonnaruva is described in the chronicles as a garden city, where King Parakrambahu I is recorded as having planted one thousand plants of every variety in the Laksa Uyana, or Park of a Thousand Trees. This obviously refers to the planting and development of the park reserves outside which surrounded the city limits, extending up to the cultivated lands and the lake.

The parks within the city are clearly named in the ancient records, and their extent can be defined by the existence of the monuments around which the park has been set out. The Nandana Uyana was the royal park set out within a walled area. The royal bath and pavilions are found

Kumara Pokuna or Royal Bath, Polonnaruva, 12th century.
The bath, a pavilion and a toilet.

immediately outside the palace wall. The Dipuyyana or Promontory Garden of Nissankamalla, located between the citadel and the lake, contained its own royal edifices. The ruins of two baths, one for swimming and the other a shallow pool, are particularly interesting. Water was brought to these baths directly from the tank by means of a sluice built for this purpose. One wonders if this sluice was also used to flood the area to form a defensive moat around the city wall.

The monasteries were included in their own parks, with avenues and terraces. It is likely that they were full of flowering trees and aromatic plants such as jasmine. Around the hospital, one can conjecture a medieval herbal garden planted with rare varieties of medicinal plants. The Hindu shrines immediately outside the city contained their own orchards with fruit trees to supply the offerings used in daily temple rituals. An inscription of Nissankamalla at the Preeti Dana Mandapa, where the king distributed alms to the poor, forbids the picking of fruits from the surrounding orchards.

We can see in Polonnaruva, a city of monastery parks, royal gardens and orchards, a continuation of the garden tradition begun in Anuradhapura and continued through the Sigiriya gardens, and the development of a garden-city concept of city planning.

The hydrological system

Legendary accounts suggest the existence of an agricultural community in and around Polonnaruva as early as the Anuradhapura period. However, it is not until the construction of tanks of Giritale, Minneriya and Kaudulla, and the smaller tanks of Polonnaruva, with their network of irrigation channels, that populous farming villages came into existence in the area. The possibility of trans-basin diversion to bring water from the perennial rivers to supplement the rainwater of the tanks was realized when the Elahera channel was cut to connect Giritale and Minneriya in the eighth century.

By the time the city of Polonnaruva came to be built and the Parakrama Samudra was created, there was already a considerable body of engineering experience in the field of hydrology in the island. The supplementary water needed for the Parakrama Samudra is provided by a channel connected to Ambanganga, a tributary of the Mahaveli. An elaborate channel system carried the water to the fields and the villages. The city of Polonnaruva had its own water supply from the tank. Water conducted along channels was stored in smaller tanks. The monastery site has several brick-built ponds, as well as miniature tanks with earthen bunds.

The breaching and consequent failure of the water storage and distribution system was probably one of the causes of the abandonment and subsequent destruction of the city. It took several centuries for the hydrological system to be reactivated. The large tank was restored and its colossal bunds and water channels repaired in the 1950s. The result of the renewed occupation of the large settlements has also affected the ancient city and its monuments. However, the Archaeological Department and, in recent years, the Cultural Triangle, have stepped in to restore and preserve the monuments as a vital link for the new settlers with their ancestral past.

Sigiriya

City, Palace and Royal Gardens

Senake Bandaranayake

One of Asia's major archaeological sites, Sigiriya presents a unique concentration of fifth-century urban planning, architecture, gardening, engineering, hydraulic technology and art. Centred on a massive rock rising 200 metres above the surrounding plain, Sigiriya's location is one of considerable natural beauty and historical interest. An area of ancient settlement lying between the historic capitals of Anuradhapura and Polonnaruva, the Sigiriya plain still retains much of its forest cover, and many of its present village settlements and man-made village reservoirs date back to the first millennium B.C. In its present form, Sigiriya itself is essentially a walled-and-moated royal capital of the fifth century A.D., with a palace complex on top of the rock, elaborate pleasure gardens, extensive moats and ramparts, and the well-known paintings on the western face of the rock.

The history of Sigiriya, however, extends from prehistoric times to the seventeenth and eighteenth centuries. The earliest evidence of human habitation is in the Aligala rock-shelter which lies to the east of the Sigiriya rock. This is a major prehistoric site of the mesolithic period, with an occupational sequence starting nearly five thousand years ago and extending up to early historic times. The historical period at Sigiriya begins about the third century B.C., with the establishment of a Buddhist monastic settlement on the rock-strewn western and northern slopes of the hill around the rock. As in other similar sites of this period, partially man-made rock-shelters or 'caves', with deeply-incised protective grooves or drip-ledges, were created in the bases of several large boulders. There are altogether 30 such shelters, many of them dated by the donatory inscriptions carved in the rock face near their drip-ledges to a period between the third century B.C., and the first century A.D. The inscriptions record the granting of these caves to the Buddhist monastic order to be used as residences.

Kasyapa, the master builder

Sigiriya comes dramatically, if tragically, into the political history of Sri Lanka in the last quarter of the fifth century during the reign of King Dhatusena I (459-477 A.D.), who ruled from the ancient capital at Anuradhapura. A palace coup by Prince Kasyapa, the King's son by a non-royal consort, and Migara, the king's nephew and army commander, led ultimately to the seizure of the throne and the subsequent execution

Rock, lake, water gardens and moats, Sigiriya, 5th century.
The western precinct of the Sigiriya Complex.

of Dhatusena. Kasyapa, much reviled for his patricide, established a new capital at Sigiriya, while the crown prince, his half-brother Moggallana, went into exile in India. Kasyapa I (477-495 A.D.) and his master-builders gave the site its present name, 'Simha-giri' or 'Lion-Mountain', and were responsible for most of the structures and the complex plan that we see today. This brief Kasyapan phase was the golden age of Sigiriya.

The post-Kasyapan phases, when Sigiriya was turned back into a Buddhist monastery, seem to have lasted until the thirteenth or fourteenth century. Sigiriya then disappears for a time from the history of Sri Lanka until, in the sixteenth and seventeenth centuries, it appears again as a distant outpost and military centre of the Kingdom of Kandy. In the mid-nineteenth century antiquarians begin to take an interest in the site, followed some decades later by archaeologists, who have now been working there for nearly 100 years, since the 1890s. The Cultural Triangle project began its work at Sigiriya in 1982 and has focussed attention not only on the best-known and most striking aspects of Sigiriya: the royal complex of rock, palace, gardens and fortifications of the 'western precinct', but also on the entire city and its rural hinterland.

Urban form

One of the most important aspects of the archaeology of Sigiriya is that it is one of the best-preserved and most elaborate surviving urban sites in South Asia from the first millennium A.D. What we know presently about its urban form is that it consists of a series of concentric precincts, the outermost of which, not yet completely surveyed, seems to form a precise geometrical rectangle. These successive precincts are centred on the great Sigiriya rock, a massive monadnock or inselberg rising about 200 metres above the surrounding plain. It has a part-natural, part man-made, stepped plateau of about 1.5 hectares on its summit. On this plateau is located the royal palace and the immediate palace gardens.

The palace stands about 360 metres above mean sea level and 200 metres above the surrounding plain. On the plain below, extending east and west, are two fortified precincts, 90 and 40 hectares in extent. Around the rock itself is a walled 'citadel' or inner royal precinct, covering an area of about 15 hectares. This citadel presents an irregular, broadly elliptical plan, more or less defining the outer limits of the hill slopes around the base of the rock. This boulder-strewn hillside has been fashioned into a series of terraces, forming a terraced garden around the rock. It also incorporates rock-shelters and rock-associated pavilions which form the distinctive architecture of the boulder gardens both to the west and the east of the citadel.

The area to the west of the citadel is laid out as a symmetrically-planned royal park or pleasure-garden with elaborate water-retaining structures and surface and sub-surface hydraulic systems. It is surrounded by three ramparts and two moats forming a rectangle whose inner dimensions are about 900 by 800 metres. To the east of the citadel extends the 'eastern precinct' or 'inner city', a rectangular form whose inner precincts measure about 700 metres from east to west and 500 metres from north to south with a high earthen rampart, gateways and vestiges of a moat. Our present

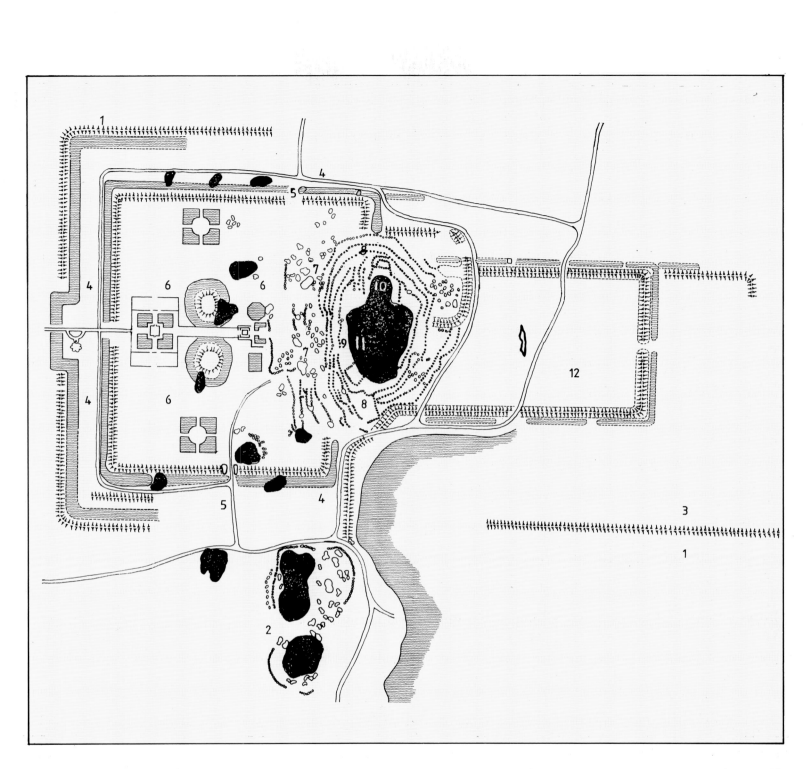

City of Sigiriya
1. Outer Moat and Rampart
2. Mapagala Complex
3. Outer City
4. Inner Moat and Rampart
5. Entrances
6. Water Gardens
7. Boulder Gardens
8. Terrace Gardens
9. Mirror Wall and Paintings
10. Lion Platform
11. Palace at the summit
12. Inner City, Ramparts and Gates

interpretation of this area is that it represents a ceremonial precinct with no permanent structures other than a large central pavilion erected on a long, low rock outcrop. The outermost rampart of the Sigiriya complex is today a low, much eroded vestigial earthen embankment defining the extent of the still largely uninvestigated eastern residential or 'outer city' area. This is more or less laid out as a rectangle, 1,000 by 1,500 metres, with two eastern gateways, suburban settlements beyond its northern walls, and the great man-made Sigiriya Lake to its south.

Among the most remarkable aspects of the urban form at Sigiriya are its planning mathematics and total design concept. The plan of the city is based on a precise square module. The layout extends outward from the coordinates at the centre of the palace complex on top of the rock. The eastern and western entrances are directly aligned with the central east-west axis. The royal water-gardens and the moats and ramparts of the western precinct are based on an 'echo' plan, which duplicates the layout on either side of the north-south and east-west axes.

In its total conception Sigiriya represents a brilliant combination of concepts of symmetry and asymmetry in a deliberate interlocking of geometrical plan and natural form.

Apsara celestial nymph, Sigiriya, 5th century. An outstanding example of the classical school of Sri Lankan painting.

The Apsara paintings

The most famous features of the Sigiriya complex are the fifth-century paintings found in a depression on the rock face more than 100 metres above ground level. Reached today by a modern spiral staircase, they are but fragmentary survivals of an immense backdrop of paintings that once extended in a wide band across the western face of the rock. The painted band seems to have extended to the north-eastern corner of the rock, covering thereby an area nearly 140 metres long and, at its widest, about 40 metres high. As John Still observed, 'The whole face of the hill appears to have been a gigantic picture gallery ... the largest picture in the world perhaps' (Still 1907: 15).

All that survives of this great painted backdrop are the female figures preserved in two adjacent depressions in the rock-face known as 'Fresco Pocket A' and 'Fresco Pocket B' (three other depressions: 'Fresco Pockets C, D and E higher up the rock-face, also contain patches of plaster and pigment and, in at least one instance, fragments of a painted figure). Traces of plaster and pigment elsewhere on the rock-face provide further evidence of the extent of the painted band. They represent *apsaras* or celestial nymphs, a common motif in the religious and royal art of Asia.

The Sigiriya paintings have been the focus of considerable interest and attention in both ancient and modern times. The poems in the graffiti on the Mirror Wall, discussed below, dating from about the sixth to the thirteenth or fourteenth century, are mostly addressed to the ladies in the paintings, who seem also to have been studied and reproduced in the eighteenth century by the Kandyan artists who painted the Dambulla murals. Antiquarian descriptions of the figures in the 'fresco pocket' date back to the 1830s. The first proper descriptions in the nineteenth century are based on the examination of the paintings by telescope from the plain below. The first person in modern times to find his way into the fresco pocket and come face to face with the paintings was an engineer named Murray of the Public Works Department. He made tracings, copied them in pastel and published a paper in 1891.

The first real study of the paintings, however, begins with the commencement of archaeological operations at Sigiriya by H.C.P. Bell from 1894 onwards and the facsimile copies in oils made by Muhandiram D.A.L. Perera in 1896-7.

Meaning and style

An important and largely unanswerable question is how the present figures related to the entire composition of the painted band extending across the rock-face. Their fragmentary nature and unusual dramatic location have led to the Sigiriya paintings being interpreted in a number of ways,

Detail from 'Fresco Pocket B', Sigiriya,
5th century.
An Apsara holds a flower in a classical
dance gesture.

sometimes quite fancifully. Of the proposals that deserve scholarly consideration the three most important ones are those of Bell, Ananda Coomaraswamy and Senerath Paranavitana.

Bell's idea that they portray the ladies of Kasyapa's court in a devotional procession to the shrine at Pidurangala is a purely imaginative reconstruction and has no precedent in the artistic and social traditions of the region or the period. It seems quite likely, however, that the court ladies and their costumes and ornaments provided models for the Sigiriya artists and that, as such, the paintings reflect the life and atmosphere, the ideals of beauty and the attitude to women, of the élite society of the time.

Paranavitana's suggestion that they represent Lightning Princesses (*vijju kumari*) and Cloud Damsels (*meghalata*) is an interpretation at once more literary and sociological. It forms part of his elaborate hypothesis, which attempts to explain Sigiriya as an expression of the cult of divine royalty, the entire palace complex being a symbolic reconstruction of the abode of the god Kuvera.

While these identifications may seem to us today an overinterpretation too specific to accept in its totality, deriving from Paranavitana's attempt to see the Sigiriya palace and royal complex primarily as an expression of divine kingship, they do draw our attention to important sociological dimensions in the understanding of ancient works of art. There is no doubt that the spatial organization and symbolism of the Sigiriya complex is profoundly determined by the cult of the king and the ideology of kingship. The great tapestry of paintings at Sigiriya, the palace on the summit and the lion staircase, are all part of a complex 'sign-language' expressing royal power and ritual status.

Coomaraswamy's identification of the Sigiriya women as apsaras is in keeping with well-established South Asian traditions and is not only the simplest but also the most logical and acceptable interpretation. Recent studies have reinforced this idea, showing that apsaras are often represented in art and literature as celestial beings who carried flowers and scattered them over kings and heroes as a celebration of victory and heroism. We can say almost with certainty that the Sigiriya ladies are celestial nymphs, very similar in essence to their successors thirteen hundred years later in the 'Daughters of Mara' panel from Dambulla, but it is also likely that they had more than one meaning and function: as expressions of royal grandeur and status and as artistic evocations of courtly life, with aesthetic and erotic dimensions.

Such an interpretation, with its varying levels of ambiguity, allows us to accommodate both Bell's and Paranavitana's suggestions at either end of a semiological spectrum. It also makes it possible for us to view the painted band at Sigiriya as a rare and early survival of a royal *citrasala*, or picture gallery, well known in Indian literature and implicit in the Culavamsa account of Parakramabahu's palaces and audience halls at Polonnaruva.

The style and authorship of the paintings have been as controversial a question as that of their identity. Early writers such as Bell, and even Coomaraswamy, saw them as extensions of the Central Indian School of Ajanta or of several related traditions such as those of Bagh or of Sittanvasal in South India. Bell even suggested that 'artists trained in the same school

'Fresco Pocket B' Sigiriya, 5th century.
It is now thought that the Sigiriya paintings
were executed in the tempera rather than true
fresco technique.

- possibly the same hands - executed both the Indian and Ceylon frescoes'. These were views expressed at a time when very little was known of the extent and character of early Sri Lankan painting.

Benjamin Rowland was amongst the first to observe carefully the actual painterly technique at Sigiriya and to note in what specific way it differed from Ajanta and other subcontinental traditions: 'The Sigiriya paintings, outside of their exciting and intrinsic beauty, are perhaps most notable for the very freedom they show at a time when the arts were tending to become more and more frozen in the mould of rigid canons of beauty. The apsaras have a rich healthy flavour that in contrast almost makes the masterpieces of Indian art seem sallow and effete in over-refinement. Just as the drawing is more vigorous than that of the more sophisticated artists of India, so colours are bolder and more intense than the tonalities employed in the temples of the Deccan' (Rowland 1938: 84).

These insights have been pursued and reinforced by contemporary Sri Lankan scholars, who rightly argue that, while the Sri Lankan paintings belong to the same broad traditions of South Asian art as the various subcontinental schools of the time, the specific character and historical continuity of the Sri Lankan tradition give it its own distinctive place in the art of the region. Thus, the Sigiriya paintings represent the earliest surviving examples of a Sri Lankan school of classical realism, already fully evolved when we first encounter it in the fifth century.

The Boulder-Garden paintings

The art of Sigiriya is not confined to the paintings on the great rock itself. Of equal archaeological and even aesthetic interest, though less well-preserved, are a number of paintings found in the rock shelters at the foot of the rock in the area that formed the boulder gardens in the time of Kasyapa. This was also the centre of both the ancient and the post-Kasyapan monasteries. Nearly thirty rock shelters and boulder arches (i.e.. archways formed of natural boulders) have been found at Sigiriya.

Significant fragments of paintings can be seen in at least five of these. Many of the others contain traces of plaster and pigment, indicating an extensive complex of painted caves and pavilions in the whole of the boulder garden area.

The most ambitious composition can be found on a large area of plaster in Cave 7 where there are faint traces of several female figures carrying flowers and moving amidst clouds, again in a northerly direction, very much like the apsaras on the main rock above. Even in ornamentation and general figural treatment, these women are broadly similar to those in the famous paintings, except for the fact that at least three of them are not cut off at the waist by clouds but are full-figure representations, with legs bent in a conventional flying posture. Altogether there are less than half a dozen distinct forms here, barely discernible in traces of body colour and linework.

The most extraordinary and certainly the most dramatic manifestations of the painter's art at Sigiriya are the remains of ceiling paintings in the rock shelter popularly known as the 'Cobra-hood Cave' (Cave 9) on account of its equally dramatic rock formation. The shelter itself dates from the

Terracotta architectural detail, Boulder Garden, Sigiriya, 5th–8th century.
This detail is typical of the moulded ornamentations of the lost brick and timber buildings in the Boulder Garden.

earliest phase of occupation at Sigiriya and bears a donatory inscription belonging to the last few centuries B.C. The painting combines geometrical shapes and motifs with a free and complex rendering of characteristic volute or whorl motifs. It is nothing less than a masterpiece of expressionist painting, displaying considerable imaginative range and artistic virtuosity in a way not seen elsewhere in the surviving paintings of the Sri Lankan tradition. The characteristic brushwork style and tonal qualities of the Sigiriya school are immediately noticeable here. There is little doubt that this awning is contemporary with the paintings on the main rock.

Further excavation in the caves of the boulder garden and detailed investigation of plaster layers and pigments will give us a much clearer idea of the successive phases of artistic activity at Sigiriya.

Considered in their totality, the paintings in the boulder-garden area at Sigiriya, though vestigial, provide important evidence of the continuation of the Sigiriya school over a fair period of time. Excavations have shown several post-fifth-century phases of occupation in the rock shelters in this area, continuing until perhaps as late as the twelfth or thirteenth century. This situation is paralleled by the layers of plaster and painting which provide evidence of several successive phases of painterly activity at Sigiriya.

The Sigiri graffiti

The Sigiriya paintings have preoccupied visitors to the site over many centuries. After the abandonment of the palace in the fifth or sixth century and the establishment of a monastery in the boulder and water garden area to the west of the rock, Sigiriya became a place of pilgrimage for visitors from all over the country, who came to see the paintings, the palace and the lion staircase. Greatly inspired by the paintings, they composed poems addressed mostly to the ladies depicted in them and inscribed their verses on the highly polished surface of the Mirror Wall just below the painting gallery. Known as the 'Sigiri graffiti' and dating from about the sixth to the early fourteenth century, hundreds of these scribbled verses cover the surface of the gallery wall and also some of the plastered surfaces in the caves below. Nearly seven hundred of these were deciphered by Paranavitana, and another 150 recently by Benille Priyanka. The poems, which express the thoughts and emotions of ancient visitors to Sigiriya, provide not only revealing comments on the paintings themselves but also an insight into the cultivated sensibilities of the time and its appreciation of art and beauty.

'Art about Art' : early souvenir sculptures

Closely connected with the paintings and the poetry are a series of miniature terracotta figurines found in the debris of collapsed structures in the Boulder Garden area on the western slopes at the base of the Sigiriya rock. These are among the most interesting archaeological finds from nearly a decade of Cultural Triangle excavations at Sigiriya. Most of the figurines appear today as female torsos, modelled in the familiar 'classic-realist' style of the Middle Historical period (circa sixth to thirteenth century). The modelling of the figurines shows a characteristic concern with three-dimensional form and a sensitivity to both anatomical and decorative detail. From their archaeological context and style we may tentatively date them to a period between the seventh and the tenth centuries. As for as we know, terracotta figures of this specific type have only been found at Sigiriya, but they are clearly related to a contemporary tradition of fine terracotta sculpture associated with other sites in the region.

What is particularly interesting is that these figures are representations or models of the famous *apsaras* of the Sigiriya paintings. The concept of the unity of sculpture and painting, i.e. the equivalence of the three-dimensional and the two-dimensional image, is a basic principle of South and Southeast Asian art. What is rare, perhaps even unique, at this early period is to find ancient works of art which are deliberate representations or, in this case, actual models or miniature reproductions of other works of art, a process which can be described as 'art about art'.

The correspondences between the paintings and the sculptures and the diminutive size of the latter (usually between 10 and 20 cm) suggest that the figurines were portable objects and not part of any fixed architectural decoration - further supporting the notion that they are models or 'souvenirs'. The production of models and souvenirs to be carried away by pilgrims visiting famous religious centres is, of course, an ancient practice, well-known in the art and archaeology of Asia. Sigiriya, however, is an example of a site, rare in the archaeological record, which seems to have been visited purely on account of its secular aesthetic and 'archaeological' attractions.

The verses are mostly addressed to the ladies in the paintings, thus, the terracotta figurines seem to have been produced as souvenirs to be taken away by visitors who appreciated the paintings. This interpretation

'Their bodies' radiance
Like the moon
Wanders in the cool wind.'

'The song of Lord Kital:
Sweet girl
Standing on the Mountain
Your teeth are like jewels
Lighting the lotus of your eyes
Talk to me gently of your heart.'

'I am Lord Sangapala
I wrote this song
We spoke
But they did not answer
Those ladies of the Mountain
They did not give us
The twitch of an eye-lid.'

'Ladies like you
Make men pour out their hearts
And you also have thrilled the body
Making its hair
Stiffen with desire.'

is preferable to one that would view the figures as decorative or iconic sculptures associated with the monastic structures amongst whose debris they occur.

The Sigiriya torsos, like the poems on the Mirror Wall, are undoubtedly an expression of 'art about art'. They interest us not only as beautiful terracotta sculptures but also as unique historical documents, supplementing the insights we gain from the poems into the society and sensibilities of the period.

The Royal Gardens

One of the major foci of the Cultural Triangle excavations has been the Sigiriya gardens. Sigiriya provides us with a unique and relatively little-known example of what is one of the oldest landscaped gardens in the world, whose skeletal layout and significant features are still in a fair state of preservation.

Three distinct but interlinked forms are found here: water gardens, cave and boulder gardens, and stepped or terraced gardens encircling the rock. A combination of these three garden types is also seen in the palace gardens on the summit of the rock.

The Water Gardens

The water gardens are, perhaps, the most extensive and intricate, and occupy the central section of the western precinct. Three principal gardens lie along the central east-west axis. The largest of these, Garden 1, consists of a central island surrounded by water and linked to the main precinct by cardinally-oriented causeways. The quartered or *char bhag* plan thus created, constitutes a well-known ancient garden form, of which the Sigiriya version is one of the oldest surviving examples. The entire garden is a walled enclosure with gateways placed at the head of each causeway. The largest of these gateways, to the west, has a triple entrance. The cavity left by the massive timber doorposts indicates that it was an elaborate gatehouse of timber and brick masonry with multiple, tiled roofs.

Garden 2, the 'Fountain Garden', is a narrow precinct on two levels. The lower, western half has two long, deep pools with stepped cross-sections. Draining into these pools are shallow serpentine 'streams' paved with marble slabs and defined kerbs. These serpentines are punctuated by fountains, consisting of circular limestone plates with symmetrical perforations. They are fed by underground water conduits and operate on a simple principle of gravity and pressure. With the cleaning and repair of the underground conduits, the fountains operate in rainy weather even today.

Two relatively shallow limestone cisterns are placed on opposite sides of the garden. Square in plan and carefully constructed, they may well have originally functioned as storage or pressure chambers for the serpentine and the fountains. The eastern half of the garden, which is raised above the western section, has few distinctive features, a serpentine stream and a pavilion with a limestone throne being almost all that is visible today.

Garden 3, on a higher level consists of an extensive area of terrace and halls. Its northeastern corner is a large octagonal pool and terrace at the

Terracotta souvenir sculpture, Sigiriya, 5th century.
Terracotta models of the painted figures on the rock.

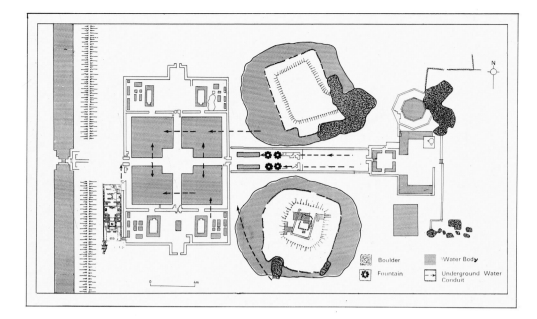

Water Garden, Sigiriya, 5th century.
The gardens in the morning mist
of the rainy season.

Water Garden at Sigiriya
1. Water Garden
2. Boulder Garden
3. Terrace Garden
4. Palace Rock

base of a towering boulder forming a dramatic juxtaposition of rock and water at the very point at which the water garden and boulder garden meet. A raised podium and a drip-ledge for a lean-to roof form the remains of a 'bathing pavilion' on the far side of the pool.

The eastern limit of Garden 3 is marked by the wide entrance and massive brick and stone wall of the citadel. The citadel wall forms a dramatic backdrop to the water gardens, echoing the even more dramatic vision of the great rock and the palace on its summit to the east. When viewed from the water gardens, the wall extends from the towering boulder of Garden 3 to a matching bastion on the south-east, formed by wide brick walls and a series of boulders which surround a cave pavilion housing a rock-cut throne.

The three water gardens form a dominant series of rectangular enclosures of varying size and character, joined together along a central east-west axis. Moving away from this to the wider conception of the western precinct as a whole, we see that its other dominant feature is a sequence of four large moated islands, arranged in a north-south oriented crescent, cutting across the central axis of the water garden. These, once again, follow the principle of symmetrical repetition, the two inner islands, on the one hand, and the two outer islands, on the other, forming pairs.

The two inner islands closely abutting the Fountain Garden on either side, are partially built up on surfacing bedrock. They are surrounded by high rubble walls and wide moats. The flattened surface of the island was occupied by 'summer palaces' (Sinhala: *sitala maliga* or cool palaces) or water pavilions. Bridges built or cut into the surface rock, provide access to these 'palaces'. Further to the north and south, almost abutting the ramparts, are the two other moated islands, still unexcavated but clearly displaying the quartered or *char bagh* plan.

Intricately connected with the water gardens of the western precinct are the double moat that surrounds it and the great artificial lake that extends southward from the Sigiriya rock. Excavations have revealed that the pools were interlinked by a network of underground conduits, fed initially by

Ancient fountains, Sigiriya, 5th century.
Fountains at play in the rainy season.

the Sigiriya Lake and probably connected at various points with the surrounding moats.

The Miniature Water Garden

To the west of Water Garden 1, recent excavations have revealed a miniature water garden very different in character from those described above.

There are at least five distinct units in this garden, each combining pavilions of brick and limestone with paved, water-retaining structures and winding water-courses. The two units at the northern and southern extremities are badly eroded, but the general layout of the major portion of the garden and of the three central units is clear.

A striking feature of this 'miniature' garden (it is in fact about ninety metres long and thirty wide) is the use of these water-surrounds with pebbled or marbled floors, covered by shallow, slowly-moving water. These, no doubt, served as a cooling device and at the same time had great aesthetic appeal, creating interesting visual and sound effects.

Another distinctive aspect is the geometrical intricacy of the garden layout. While displaying the symmetry and 'echo-planning' characteristic of the water-gardens as a whole, this miniature garden has a far more complex interplay of tile-roofed buildings, water-retaining structures and water-courses than is seen elsewhere in Sigiriya; even more intricate, in fact, than the beautiful 'Fountain Garden'.

Miniature Water Garden, Sigiriya, 5th century. This refined garden layout retains various paved ponds using pebble and marble floors with slow moving water.

Rock cut footings, Sigiriya, 5th century.
These cuttings on the rock were meant as
foundations for brick masonry.

This newly-discovered garden seems to belong to more than one phase of construction. As far as we are able to say at this stage of our investigation, the garden seems originally to have been laid out as an extension and 'miniaturized' refinement of the Kasyapan macro-plan and therefore belongs in essence to the last quarter of the fifth century. But it seems to have been added to later and remodelled and then finally abandoned and again partially built over in the last phases of the post-Kasyapan period, between the tenth and thirteenth centuries.

It seems very likely that a similar garden lies buried beneath the lawns of the unexcavated parallel sector in the northern half of the water-gardens, an 'echo' or 'twin' of the present garden in the south.

The Boulder Garden

The boulder garden presents a garden design which is in marked contrast to the symmetry and geometry of the water gardens. It is an entirely organic or symmetrical conception, consisting of a number of winding pathways, which link several clusters of large natural boulders extending from the southern slopes of the Sigiriya hill to the northern slopes below the plateau of the lion staircase. One of the most striking features of this boulder garden is the way in which almost every rock and boulder had a building or pavilion set upon it. What seem to us today like steps and drains or a honeycomb of holes on the sides or tops of boulders, are in fact the foundations or footings of ancient brick walls and of timber columns and beams.

Among the unusual features of the garden are the *impluvium* of the 'Cistern Rock', taking its name from a large cistern formed out of massive slabs of granite, and the 'Audience Hall Rock' which has a flattened summit and a large 5-metre long throne carved out of the living rock. The honeycomb of post-holes and flattened ledges of the 'Preaching Rock' are others. While considerable excavation will have to be done before we can recover the original pathways of the boulder garden, at least two distinct

Moat of the Summer Palace, Sigiriya,
5th century.
The southern Summer Palace is one of five
moated islands in the water gardens at Sigiriya.

markers are provided by two 'boulder arches' and limestone staircases, as well as various flights of steps and passageways constructed of polished marble blocks and slabs. The vertical 'drains' cut in the sides of rocks in a few places indicates that, water-courses and controlled water movement formed part of the garden architecture in this area too.

The Terraced Gardens

The third garden form at Sigiriya, the terraced gardens have been fashioned out of the natural hill at the base of the Sigiriya rock by the construction of a series of rubble-retaining walls, each terrace rising above the other and running in a roughly concentric plan around the rock.

The great brick-built staircases with limestone steps traverse the terrace gardens on the west, connecting the pathways of the boulder garden to the precipitous sides of the main Sigiriya rock itself. From here, a covered ambulatory or gallery provides access to the belly of the rock to what is in effect the uppermost terrace, the 'Lion Staircase plateau', with its chambers, buildings and pavilions and the great lion itself.

The Mirror Wall

The Mirror Wall dates from the fifth century and has been substantially preserved in its original form. Built up from the base of the rock itself with brick masonry, the wall has a highly polished plaster finish, from which it gets its ancient name, the Mirror Wall. The wall encloses a walk or gallery paved with polished marble slabs. The famous Sigiriya paintings are found in a depression high above this gallery. The polished inner surface of the mirror wall contains the Sigiriya Graffiti as described above.

The Lion Staircase

One of Sigiriya's most dramatic features is its great Lion Staircase, now preserved only in two colossal paws and a mass of brick masonry surrounding the ancient limestone steps.

*Lion Staircase, Sigiriya, 5th century.
A masterpiece of the bricklayer's
and plasterer's art.*

The lion, so impressive even in its ruined state today, must have afforded a vision of grandeur and majesty when it was intact. Remarkably, we have poems recording the impact of the Lion on ancient visitors to the site.

'The monstrous *Simha* — suggestive of the legendary founder of the Sinhalese race — towering majestically against the granite cliff, bright-coloured, and gazing northwards over a vista that stretches almost hill-less to the horizon, must have presented an awe-inspiring sight for miles around. (H.C.P. Bell 1904: 9)

We know from the chronicle account of Kasyapa's construction of Sigiriya that the Lion Staircase House was one of the principle features of his plan of the Sigiriya complex. The Lion was in effect the ultimate and solitary gatehouse to the palace on the summit.

*The Lion Staircase and the palace on the summit,
Sigiriya, 5th century.
The lion staircase was the main gateway to the
palace on the summit.*

At the same time it made a major symbolic statement, operating on several levels of meaning, enhancing the power and majesty of royal authority and invoking ritual notions of dynastic origins, the Lion being the mythical ancestor and the royal symbol of the Sri Lankan Kings.

The actual structure of the Lion Staircase House itself can be at least partially reconstructed from the evidence still remaining at the site. The

*Palace, Lion Staircase, Garden and Lake,
Sigiriya, 5th century.
A panoramic view of the centre of the Sigiriya
complex, with the Terrace and Boulder Garden
in the foreground and the lake in the distance.
(overleaf)*

paws, the surving masses of brick masonry and the original limestone risers give us a clear idea of the form, scale and materials used in the construction of the Lion: basically a brick masonry structure with its surface moulded fairly realistically in a thick coating of lime plaster. The Lion seems to have been in a crouching position, represented by its paws, head and shoulders projecting from the rock. The exact width and height of the Lion is indicated by cuts and grooves in the rock-face. It is likely that timber posts, beams and lintels were used inside the brick masonry to create the passages for the stairs, the decay of this timber framework leading ultimately to the collapse of a substantial part of the entire structure.

The Lion Staircase House stood to a height of fourteen metres. Above this the gently-sloping rockface was utilized once again to erect a gently ascending gallery and staircase, presumably of brick masonry with stone risers.

The Palace

The summit of the Sigiriya rock is in the form of a stepped plateau with a total extent of more than 1.5 hectares.

The palace was the centre of the royal city. Lying abut 180m above the surrounding plain and 360 m above mean sea level at its highest point, it is not only the loftiest and inner-most precinct of the Sigiriya complex, but it is also the geometrical centre of the ancient modular grid on which

The palace on the summit, Sigiriya, 5th century. A view from the south.

*Rock pool on summit, Sigiriya, 5th century.
This rock-cut pool was the central feature of the
palace gardens on the summit.*

the plan of Sigiriya is based. The central north-south and east-west axes of the entire complex intersect near the mid-point of the palace area.

The earliest surviving palace in Sri Lanka, with its layout and basic ground plan still clearly visible, it provides important comparative data for the study of Asian palace forms.

The palace complex divides into three distinct parts: the outer or lower palace occupying the lower eastern part of the summit; the inner or upper palace occupying the high western section, and the palace gardens to the south. The three sectors converge on a large and beautiful rock-cut pool bordered on two sides by a stone-flagged pavement. A marble-paved walk runs down the centre of the complex between the outer and the inner palace, forming an axial north-south corridor.

*Sigiriya territory with Buddhist monasteries,
village tanks and major iron producing centres.
1. Sigiriya city.
2. Pidurangala monastery.
3. Ramakale monastery.
4. Talkote settlement complex.
5. Alakolavava iron-production site.
6. Sigiri Mahavava.*

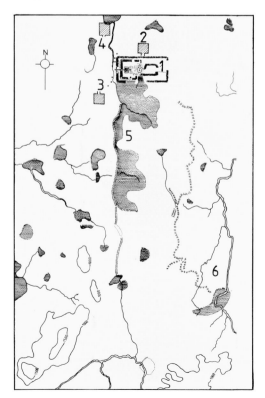

The Sigiriya Hinterland

The archaeology of the Sigiriya complex is not limited to the palace, the gardens and the city, but extends to a large hinterland known in ancient times as the 'Sihagiri Bim', the Sigiri Territory. Recent archaeological explorations have shown that this area presents a complex archaeological landscape consisting of a large number of rural settlement sites, village tanks, protohistoric cemeteries, major iron-producing centres, and a variety of Buddhist monasteries. The immediate greater Sigiriya area includes suburban settlements outside the city walls and along the Sigiri Oya. A major irrigation network to the south of the Sigiriya rock is formed by the Sigiri Mahavava, a great man-made lake more than eight kilometres in length, and the twelve - kilometre long Vavala canal network. Immediately to the north and south of the city are the ancient fortress of Mapagala, with its 'Cyclopean' walls, dating from the first to the third centuries A.D., and the major monastery complexes of Pidurangala and Ramakale. Recent studies of this remarkable landscape have made it one of the most intensively surveyed archaeo-historical micro-regions in South Asia.

Dambulla

The Golden Mountain temple

Senake Bandaranayake

The Buddhist monastery at Dambulla, the ancient Jambukola vihara, is best known for its rock temples and its great cycle of well-preserved eighteenth–century rock and wall paintings. It is one of the largest cave temple complexes in the South and Southeast Asian region and one of the most important centres of Buddhist pilgrimage in Sri Lanka. Dambulla is also an extremely complex archaeological and historical site, a palimpsest reflecting successive periods of human occupation, with a history extending from prehistoric and protohistoric times right down to the modern period.

Rock and Upper Terrace, Dambulla, 3rd century B.C. and later.
The upper terrace at Dambulla had been in continuous use for more than two thousand years.

Located near the centre of Sri Lanka, at the northern edge of the central mountains as they descend to the great plains of the north-central Dry Zone, the Dambulla rock has been formed by the combination of two great rock outcrops, erosional remnants or inselbergs, each roughly domical in shape. Like Sigiriya, they are of considerable importance and interest in the study of the geological history of Sri Lanka.

From historical times to the present day, Dambulla has played an important role in the communication system of the northern half of the country. It functions as a radial hub or nodal point between the eastern and western sections of the Dry Zone and also as a gateway from the Dry Zone plains to the central mountains. This location, its distinctive topography and its surrounding natural resources have made Dambulla an important focus of human activity through various historical periods. Added to this is the extraordinary and unspoilt natural beauty of the site, with its massive rocks interspersed with deeply-forested tracts.

Prehistory and the first farmers

Along the western slopes of the Dambulla rock is a series of large boulders, terraces and caves, which formed the habitat of prehistoric man. Excavations on the uppermost terrace of the Dambulla complex have yielded remains of prehistoric stone implements, displaced from the rock shelters when they were cleaned out in Early Historic times. They are the first indications

Rock of Dambulla
1. Modern settlement
2. Peripheral proceesional path
3. Pilgrim path
4. Residences of monks
5. Old cave residences
6. The five painted cave shrines
7. Summit

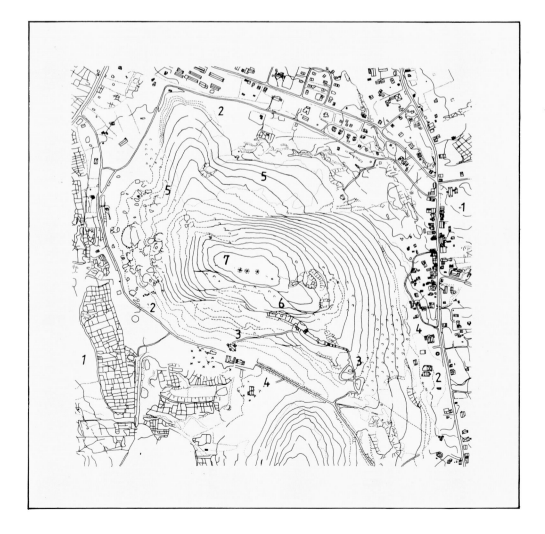

we have of a process of successive waves of human activity at Dambulla, when one historical period overtakes another, leaving some signs or remains of its predecessors behind. These prehistoric remains make Dambulla one of a small and rare group of recently identified prehistoric rock-shelter sites in the northern Dry Zone.

Prehistoric man was succeeded by the first settlers and farmers of the protohistoric period at some time durng the first millenium B.C. Dambulla is surrounded by a number of megalithic cemeteries and protohistoric and early historic settlements. The best known of these is Ibbankatuva, which seems to be closely linked to the Dambulla complex. The megalithic cemetery at Ibbankatuva is one of the largest in the country. Two of its 42 clusters of megalithic tombs have been excavated and conserved, yielding a rich body of information about the beginnings of iron-age farming in the area. Early settlement sites on the bank of the Dambulu Oya, the Dambulla river, are amongst the oldest village and proto-urban settlements discovered in Sri Lanka so far, which throw significant light on the rural base of Sri Lanka's classical civilization. It seems likely that major settlements such as Ibbankatuva formed the social and economic infrastructure which sustained the early Buddhist monastery at Dambulla and that the titled donors of the monastic rock-shelter residences were from amongst the elite of these hinterland farming communities.

Rock ceiling, Ambulatory, Maharaja Vihara, Dambulla, 18th and 19th centuries.
Curved rock ceiling of the ambulatory with 19th century paintings.

Sculpture and Painting, Maharaja Vihara, Dambulla, 18th and 19th centuries.
Seated, standing and recumbent images of the Buddha. In the foreground are ceiling paintings depicting 1000 Buddhas.

The early monastery

Thus, the protohistoric period at Dambulla merges with the early historic one. At some time around the third century B.C., the western and southern rockface and the surrounding boulder area become the location for one of the largest early Buddhist monastic settlements in the island. The area from the upper terrace downwards to the south and west contains 73 rock shelter residences. These early rock shelters are marked by drip-ledged caves and donatory inscriptions carved above the drip-ledge. It is the uppermost group of rock shelters on the southern face of the Dambulla rock that continued into the subsequent historical period as the ritual and artistic centre of the Dambulla complex.

Since its founding in the third century B.C., this upper terrace seems to have been in continuous occupation for more than twenty-two centuries right down to the present day. Remains of many successive periods of use are visible today. The five cave temples contain an internal area of about 1,000 square metres and constitute one of the largest complexes of ancient cave or rock-shelter architecture in the South and South-East Asian region. They can be compared with major Indian sites such as Ajanta, Elura or Karle, but belong to an entirely different type, consisting of a deeply excavated cavity extending into the rock face, with screen walls in front and a lean-to roof. This is a distinctively Sri Lankan expression of a broad South Asian temple concept and has few parallels elsewhere. Dambulla is undoubtedly the largest, the most dramatic, the best-preserved and the most integrated example of this type of Buddhist vihara in Sri Lanka.

The central shrines of the Dambulla complex have been formed out of a deep cavern, part natural, part excavated, more than halfway up the western slope of the rock. Screen walls and partitions have created a number of separate chambers, of which five are in use today, each

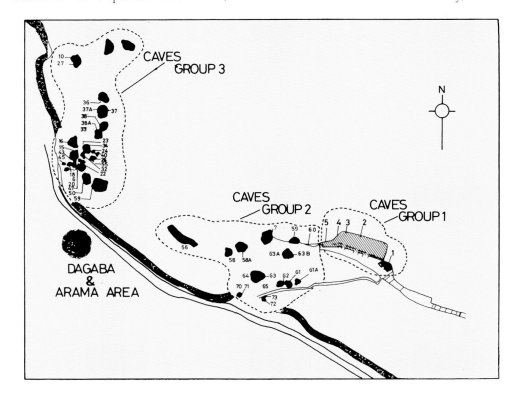

Characteristic cave layout in clusters.
1. Group 1
2. Group 2
3. Group 3

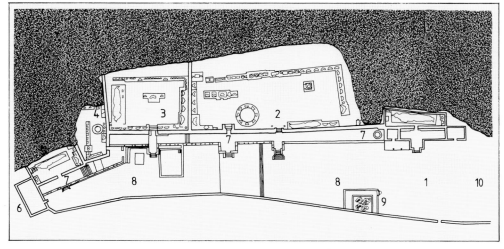

constituting an independent shrine. The largest of these, Vihara 2, is known as the *Maharaja Vihara* after its traditional founder, Valagamba or Vattagamani Abhaya (103 and 89-77 B.C.), a king of the Anuradhapura dynasty associated in popular belief with nearly all the ancient rock-shelter sites in the country. Its drip-ledge still bears an ancient inscription in Early Brahmi characters, testifying to its establishment in the reign of 'Gamini Tisa', and thought to refer to Vattagamani Abhaya. Thirty-six other donatory inscriptions of this period have been found in association with the drip-ledged rock shelters.

During the Middle Historical Period (c. fifth to thirteenth century A.D.), Dambulla continued to develop as a major religious centre. The ancient residential rock shelters on the upper terrace were converted into shrines. These retained the original drip-ledges of the early period but now took the form of deep rock temples, with large screen walls of adobe or brick masonry and elaborate entrances, forming a façade whose details we can no longer conjecture, but whose broad plan and basic structural principles are echoed in what we see at the site today. Documentary and archaeological evidence, such as the fragments of painting remaining below the drip-ledge of Vihara 3 dating from between the fifth and the seventh centuries, shows that after their original founding, the Dambulla viharas were in use through the early and middle historical Period. We know from inscriptional records at the site and from documentary records that the temples were refurbished at the end of the twelfth century and again in the reign of King Senarat (1604-35), before their complete restoration and repainting in the eighteenth century.

The Maharaja Vihara

The architectural masterpiece of the Dambulla complex is the Maharaja Vihara, which has been formed by the addition of screen walls and partitions to the central section of the great cavern referred to above. Extending about 52 metres from east to west, and 23 metres deep, it has a maximum height of seven metres near the main screen wall. Two doors give entry to the shrine from a wide, galleried verandah. Its vast interior, one of the most dramatic internal spaces in Sri Lankan architecture, is not compartmented, but is spatially differentiated by a complex arrangement of statues and paintings.

Facade of the five caves, Dambulla.
These caves were lived in since the 3rd century B.C.,and renovated from time to time. (overleaf)

Despite the absence of architectural divisions, a loosely defined but clearly observable system of spatial zoning and hierarchy exists within this elaborately painted and sculptured space. The iconography of the shrine divides it into three distinct areas: the central sanctuary in front of the principal Buddha image, with its *makara torana* and attendant deities, is flanked by two subsidiary areas to the east and west, one surmounted by a large panel of narrative registers painted on its ceiling and the other by a small, rock-cut stupa, surrounded by eight seated Buddha images. Moving further east, we find an extension or 'antechamber' to this central sanctuary, in the form of a hall or subsidiary sanctum, covering a large, relatively open space. Its limits are defined by the *dagaba* and central sanctuary on the west, rows of Buddha images to the north and east, and a large, recumbent image to the south. This area can be entered directly from the southern doorway or from the central sanctuary. In the centre of the eastern section of this antechamber area is a small, half-walled precinct, in which a large vessel is placed to collect water dripping from the ceiling of the cave, the water believed to have sacred properties and used in daily temple offerings.

On an entirely different level of ritual importance is a recess in the south-eastern corner of the shrine behind the eastern row of seated Buddhas, guarded by a royal portrait statue traditionally identified as being

Central sanctuary, Maharaja Vihara, Dambulla, 18th century.
Miniature stupa and principal Buddha image. The ceiling painting in the foreground depicts the first sermon of the Buddha.

Sculpture of King Nissankamalla,
Maharaja Vihara, Dambulla, 18th century.
One of three royal portrait sculptures at
Dambulla.

that of King Nissankamalla. This forms a kind of entrance to an outer passage or 'ambulatory' running behind the row of seated images and connecting the southern recess with the northern extremity of the chamber. These three major elements form a total conception which displays an intricate plan, whose spatial divisions are both defined and reinforced by the arrangement and iconography of the paintings and sculptures as the accompanying plans show.

Stupa, Bodhighara and assembly hall

An important development of the middle historical period was the expansion of the Dambulla vihara to an elaborate architectural complex at the foot of the rock in the south western sector, excavated and conserved under the Cultural Triangle programme. These investigations have given us a great deal of information about the evolutionary history of Dambulla in the period between the fifth and thirteenth centuries. They have also considerably added to the range of monuments that can be seen at Dambulla. We also have a very good idea of the different phases of

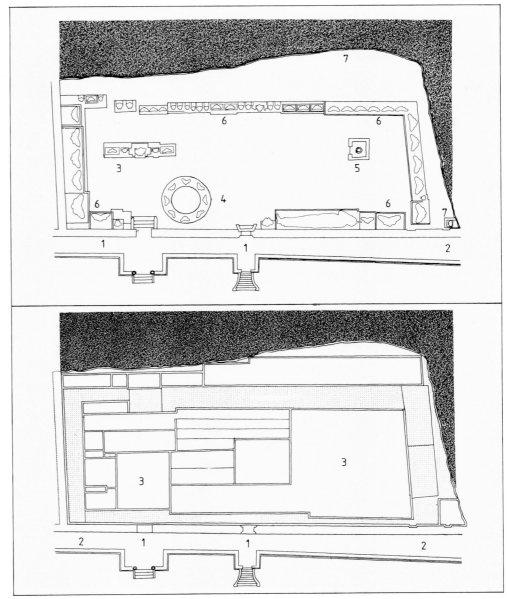

Plan of Cave No. 2.
1. Entrances
2. Varandah
3. Main image
4. Stupa
5. Holy water drip
6. Buddha images
7. Ambulatory

constructional activity at this site by studying the remains of the ancient *stupa* and the *Bodhighara* (i.e. Bodhi-tree temple) found here.

During the latter part of the Middle Historic Period, at the end of the twelfth century, Dambulla was visited by King Nissankamalla, who left an elaborate inscription on the rock face. He is recorded as having been responsible for establishing new rock temples and commissioning the sculpture in the Devaraja Vihara (Vihara 1, the 'Vihara of the King of the Gods', the first of the five cave temples on the upper terrace at Dambulla).

Dambulla and the Kings of Kandy

Towards the end of the Late Historical Period, in the seventeenth and eighteenth centuries, Dambulla once again becomes a centre of major royal and religious activity. In keeping with longstanding traditions, the entire upper terrace complex is restored and refurbished during the revival of Buddhism and Buddhist art in the reign of Kirti Srirajasimha (1747-82). The five main rock temples are entirely repainted or over-painted in the post-classic style of the central Kandyan school of the late eighteenth century.

The Dambulla cycle

It is these eighteenth century murals that form the most important artistic heritage of Dambulla. They cover an area of more than 2,000 square metres, spread over the five shrines. The largest of these is Vihara 2, which is an elaborate complex of paintings, sculpture and architecture and one of the most ambitious undertakings of the Kandyan artists. The murals at Dambulla are the largest preserved group of rock and wall paintings in the region, after the cycle of ancient paintings at the Indian site of Ajanta. They are also one of the finest examples of Late Historical Period murals belonging to a pan-regional tradition that extends across South and Southeast Asia, especially in Southern India, Sri Lanka, Burma and Thailand. Dambulla is undoubtedly one of the finest and most impressive expressions of this tradition.

Rock and wall paintings

The Dambulla paintings as a whole display an enormous variety of style and subject matter. The great *Mara Parajaya* ('Defeat of Mara') panel resembles similar compositions at Degaldoruva or Danakirigala, while the *Isipatana* panel, with its exquisite craftsmanship in the treatment of the nimbus around the Buddha and the elegance and variety of its massed gods and goddesses, is rarely matched elsewhere in Kandyan art. This last is, in more ways than one, the equivalent in late-period painting of the rows of devas in the *antarala* of the Tivanka temple at Polonnaruva, while the celestial damsels of the neighbouring 'Daughters of Mara' panel are a Kandyan painter's version of the Sigiriya *apsaras*.

Dambulla, in common with some other eighteenth-century Kandyan temples, has no *jataka* stories, except for a scene representing *Jataka* paintings in the relic-chamber of the Ruvanvalisaya at Anuradhapura as it was described in the chronicles. However, three sets of 'continuous narrative' paintings are found here: the *Buddha Carita* registers in the main chamber,

Army of God Mara, Maharaja Vihara, Dambulla, 18th century.
A large variety of characters are depicted as soldiers.

Scenes from Sri Lankan history, Maharaja Vihara, Dambulla, 18th century.
They include the arrival of King Vijaya the introduction of Buddhism to Sri Lanka and other important events.

The First Sermon of the Buddha, Maharaja Vihara, Dambulla, 18th century.
One of the great panel compositions, a masterpiece of the central Kandyan school of the 18th century. (overleaf)

146

147

and the 'Arrival of Vijaya' and 'Advent of Buddhism' sequences in the southern recess. All other narrative themes are based on the centralized composition technique, the larger panels in a monumental style and the smaller ones using a modified and looser version of this. The murals in the ambulatory are exceptional, and consist of 'set piece' compositions such as the battle between Kings Dutthagamani and Elara, and the Ruvanvalisaya scene with its Jataka paintings.

The limpid and elegant draughtsmanship of some of the best scenes from the *Buddha Carita* registers belong firmly within the central Kandyan style, and are entirely different in feeling from the confident and vigorous renderings of the same style in the 'Advent of Buddhism' murals in the recess. Other *Buddha Carita* panels, such as the Parinirvana and cremation scenes, are less carefully drawn and have something of the quality of provincial painting or late manifestations of the central style. The Vijayan sequence, especially the representation of a lotus pond in which Vijaya's companions are bathing, is an unusually free composition, using the decorative language of Kandyan painting for a narrative purpose. The ambulatory murals, on the other hand, are even more unusual, with their nearly life-size proportions and free and varied use of the portrait and hieratic styles for narrative composition.

A degree of overpainting or repainting is also found in Vihara 2, as in the other shrines at Dambulla. Clear examples of this are the *arhat* figures behind the principal Buddha image and the turbanned attendant beside the Nissankamalla statue. This is even more extensive in Viharas 3 and 4. The great celestial palaces in these two shrines, especially that on the ceiling of Vihara 3, are some of the largest, most impressive and most architecturally informative expressions of this subject in Kandyan painting, although at least some of them have been been completely retouched or repainted in more recent times. Those in Vihara 4 display a basically eighteenth–century design with the characteristic polychromy of the transitional period (c.1890-1930).

Temptation of the Buddha by the Daughters of Mara, Maharaja Vihara, Dambulla, 18th century.
The female figures are represented as apsaras or celestial nymphs.

The first council after the demise of the Buddha, Maharaja Vihara, Dambulla, 18th century.
The two relegious leaders Ven. Mahakassapa and Ven. Ananda are seen seated on raised thrones.

Arhat, Maharaja Vihara, Dambulla, 19th century.
A painted figure.

A provincial or folk style of the nineteenth century is apparent on the screen wall of Vihara 3, while tracery and decorative motifs of the early twentieth century are noticeable in and around many of the Buddha images in all the shrines. Vihara 5, which was almost entirely repainted in 1905, provides an interesting example of the provincial Kandyan style in one of its latest dated survivals.

Our imperfect understanding of stylistic variations in eighteenth-century painting in general, and the subsequent additions and restorations to the paintings at Dambulla, makes the identification of a chronological sequence of styles here an uncertain task. However, the following tentative sequence is proposed:

The great centralized panel compositions and the *sat sati* panels belong to a single group, and are clear expressions of the central Kandyan style of the 1770s and 1780s.

The smaller panels illustrating the life of the Buddha after his first sermon, and his *Parinirvana*, are in a looser rendering of the same compositional method but of uneven artistic quality and with considerable stylistic variation within the group.

The narrative style of the *Buddha Carita* registers depicting the period before the *Mara parajaya* and Enlightenment are in a typical eighteenth-century narrative style.

All these three groups in the central sanctum area, which were planned and probably executed during the same period, must date from the reign of Kirti Srirajasimha. The *Nilagama Tudapata* ascribes these paintings to the reign of that king, but refers to them again in connection with Sri Vickramarajasimha. We can reasonably assume that this indicates only some repairs or retouching, or perhaps the completion or repainting of some of the panels in Group 2.

The 'Thousand Buddhas' sequence is again ascribed in the *Nilagama Tudapata* to both kings, and therefore possibly represents an early nineteenth-century restoration, as do the narrative registers in the recess which are clearly assigned in the chronicle to the reign of Sri Vikrama Rajasimha, and probably represent the early nineteenth-century continuation of the eighteenth-century narrative style.

The latest paintings in this sequence are the large 'set pieces', or historical compositions of the ambulatory.

The paintings in Viharas 3 and 4 are also in a basically eighteenth-century style, confirming the *Nilagama Tudapata* account, but most of the paintings in Vihara 4 have been heavily repainted, probably in the early decades of the present century.

The numerous *arhats* and other hieratic figures in Vihara 2 may be ascribed to the early nineteenth century; again, on stylistic grounds as well as on the basis of the *sannasa* descriptions.

The elaborate landscape composition featuring the cosmic Himalayan lake, the *Anotaptavila*, on the inner face of the screen wall of Vihara 3, seen to the right as one enters the chamber, is in a nineteenth-century provincial folk style.

The polychrome tracery and other ornamental detailing applied to awnings, decorative creeper motifs, and especially the pillows of recumbent Buddha images in Viharas 2 and 3 date from the 1890s to the 1930s.

The paintings in Vihara 5 were completed in 1915.

The most recent paintings, executed in the mid-twentieth century, include the eastern wall of Vihara 1, as well as the repainting of the nimbuses and throne backdrops of many of the seated Buddha images in Viharas 2 and 3.

Despite this long sequence of nearly two hundred years of painting at Dambulla, it is significant that the main body of eighteenth-century rock and wall-painting, especially in Viharas 2 and 3, has remained untouched and in a relatively good state of preservation. Although the temple suffered many vicissitudes, particularly in the mid-nineteenth century, when it was for a time one of the principal centres of anti-colonial resistance and rebellion, its abbots and monks have preserved the character and integrity of the ancient site, and the largest single cycle of late-period paintings available to us today. Like Sigiriya for the early period, Dambulla constitutes a source-book and a focal centre for the study and appreciation of the Kandyan tradition.

Sculpture

Dambulla has also one of the richest collections of Sri Lankan sculpture in the form of a large number of Buddha images in standing, seated and

A floral motif, Dambulla, 18th century. Many designs of floral patterns are seen incorporated into the painted surfaces.

recumbent postures as well as a few outstanding figures of gods and *Bodhisattvas* and three rare royal portrait sculptures. A large number of these images date from the Middle Historical Period, (cerea fifth to eighth century A.D.), but many of these have been restored or remodelled in the eighteenth and nineteenth centuries, although their original styles, detail and iconography have been substantially preserved. A number of new sculptural elements has also been added during the Kandyan period and in more recent times, but follows the traditions of the classic period. The excavations at Dambulla have also revealed terracotta sculpture of high quality which, together with the fragments of early painting found just below the ancient drip-ledge of Vihara 3, give us an indication of the rich fabric of artistic production during the early centuries of the Middle Historical Period.

The richest ensemble of sculpture at Dambulla, like the paintings, is found in the great Maharaja Vihara. The main entrance to this shrine, from the south, leads directly to the principal Buddha image and *makara torana*, both fashioned out of the natural rock and flanked by the Bodhisattva Maitreya and the god Natha, and also by two seated Buddhas. Behind the main image are statues of Saman and Visnu/Upulvan, two of

Principal Buddha image, Vihara No. 3, Dambulla, 18th century.
The main image in Vihara No.3 is a seated figure of the Buddha under a makara torana.

the four guardian gods of Lanka, as well as painted representations of the gods Skanda/Kataragama and the elephant-headed Ganesa. A long line of Buddha images, possibly representing the previous Buddhas, extends eastwards, dominating the northern and eastern extensions of the shrine. At the western end, four other seated images face the chamber and are thought to be the four most recent Buddhas, Kakusanda, Konagama, Kasyapa and Gautama; to the right as we face the main image is a rock-cut *dagaba* with eight directionally-oriented Buddha images, while to the right of the southern door is a recumbent Buddha image, dating from the late nineteenth or early twentieth century. Two royal portrait figures, one traditionally associated with the founder king Vatthagamani Abhaya and the other with Nissankamalla, who visited Dambulla and repaired and restored the temple in the twelfth century, are located at the western and eastern ends of the vihara respectively.

The centrepiece of Vihara 3, an outstanding example of eighteenth-century Kandyan sculpture, is the main Buddha image seated on a seat or throne decorated with lion motifs, and surrounded by a *makara torana* executed in the elaborate polychrome detailing of the central Kandyan tradition. This vihara also contains the third royal portrait sculpture at

Principal Buddha image and attendant sculptures, Maharaja Vihara, Dambulla, 9th-12th centuries.
Principal icon in the centre sanctuary, cut out of the living rock.

Dambulla, an unusual nineteenth-century full - figure sculpture of King Kirti Srirajasimha, standing against a painted mural backdrop depicting a cloth hanging and royal attendants.

The combination of early and later period sculptures in the five viharas at Dambulla is a very good example of how, in a living tradition, new sculptural elements are added to an existing ensemble without obscuring or interfering with the integral character of the older sculptural forms. This is similar to the way in which the screen walls were rebuilt or restored, or a roofed outer verandah and an arcaded facade were added in modern times, in a form probably broadly similar to that known to have existed here in the eighteenth and nineteenth centuries.

Nineteenth and early twentieth century

With the collapse of the last independent Sri Lankan kingdom in 1815, Dambulla lost its royal patronage and also, during the mid-nineteenth century, became for a time the centre of anti-colonial resistance. However, despite the setbacks resulting from this situation, the Dambulla complex retained its palimpsest of various historical periods and especially the integrity of its penultimate eighteenth-century developments.

The sculptures were periodically repainted maintaining a traditional practice. The artists in charge of this refurbishment were hereditary master craftsmen, the direct descendants of the eighteenth-century masters. The present generation of these painters are still active at the temple today and have been incorporated in the modern team of mural conservators working at the site in the Cultural Triangle mural conservation programme. The nineteenth - and twentieth - century interventions at Dambulla have not affected the eighteenth - century paintings. With the exception of the small Vihara No. 5, which was repainted in 1915, at least eighty per cent of the original eighteenth–century murals remain intact, protected by the rock ceiling and the fairly well-sealed and well-ventilated interiors of the viharas. It is only where water damage has affected the murals that nineteenth-century or early/mid-twentieth-century repainting has been carried out. An important portrait sculpture of the mid-nineteenth century shows the continuity of the sculptural tradition. This is a portrait of the eighteenth-century King who commissioned the murals, executed perhaps 50 or 100 years after the event, indicating how Dambulla was always conscious of its historical continuities and its transformations. Earlier portrait sculptures are identified with patrons who lived 2,000 or 1,000 years ago (portraits of 'Valagamba' and of Nissankamalla).

The last cycle of paintings is from 1915, when Vihara 5 was repainted on the basis of a commission by a local nobleman. It is still in a provincial version of the traditional eighteenth-century style.

The final additions to Dambulla were the construction of the verandah facades by the abbot of the complex in the 1930s, in a style which is a mixture of European and Asian detailing, deployed in a manner typical of Asian transitional architecture from the late nineteenth to early twentieth century.

Kandy

The historic hill capital

Nimal de Silva

The last capital of the Sinhala kings, Kandy is remarkable for the natural beauty of its setting in a peaceful wooded valley overlooking a vast artificial lake. The palace buildings, shrines and the British period buildings give it a special character, while the religious importance of the Tooth Relic and the annual procession of the *Dalada Perahera* contribute a dynamism and unique cultural importance to the historic hill capital.

Numerous references found in the *Mahavamsa*, the great chronicle of the Sinhalese, and in the Brahmi inscriptions found on Kandyan sites dating from the beginning of the Christian era, reveal a long-standing

Historic city, Kandy.
The city is positioned between the Udavattakele forest and the Kandy lake. These were the natural defences of the city.

occupation of the Kandy region, but it is not until the downfall of the two great kingdoms of Anuradhapura and Polonnaruva, when the capital city, along with the royal residence, was moved to the hill country, that the area comes into historical focus. With the establishment of Gampola as the capital, great importance was given to establishing a religious settlement in its suburbs. King Vikramabahu III (1357-74 A.D.) of Gampola built a shrine, the Nathadevale, dedicated to the God Lokesvara Natha, in Senkadagalapura. This is the oldest extant structure in Kandy.

The *Asgiriya Talpata*, a historical record documenting the history of the Asgiriya Monastery in Kandy, relates how General Siri Vardhana, a nephew of King Panditha Parakramabahu IV (1302-26), founded the city of Senkadagala Sirivardhanapura on the site of the former city of Katupula. In 1312, the great King founded a hermitage for the monks in the city and named it Asgiri Viharaya. According to the chronicles, the city originated at the beginning of the fourteenth century, becoming a city of royal residence under King Vikramabahu III. A century later, King Sena Sammata Vikramabahu (1469-1511) established Senkadagalapura as the capital of the Kandyan Kingdom.

The 130-year reign of the first three kings in Kandy, Sena Sammata Vikramabahu, Jayaveera (1511-51) and Karaliyadde Bandara (1551-81), ended with the conquest of Sitavaka by Rajasimha I (1554-93).

King Vimaladharmasuriya (1590-1604) founded the second dynasty years with their nine kings, the last of whom was Sri Vikramarajasimha (1798-1815). The 133 years of British occupation ended with the independence of Sri Lanka in 1948. The city of Senkadagalapura, or Kandy as it was called by Europeans, has played an extremely important role in the political and cultural history of Sri Lanka.

A natural fortress

The geographical location of Kandy was very important in creating a natural defense strategy. The city was built in a valley surrounded by three mountain ranges: Udawattakele to the east, the Hantana range on one side and the Bahiravakanda range on the other. The river Mahaveli, flowing towards the north-west, turns back on itself towards the south-west, forming a triangular boundary. This natural system of defense was very useful in protecting the city from many attempted invasions by the Portuguese, Dutch and British. The strategic principles evolved as methods of defense in planning cities in the East were fulfilled by the natural barriers of mountains (*giri durga*), water (*jala durga*), forests (*vana durga*) and marshes (*panka durga*). Notwithstanding, during certain critical periods, the kings of Kandy had to built cities like Aluthnuvara, Medamahanuvara, Hanguranketanuvara, Nillambenuvara, Kundasalenuvara and Galenuvara and were obliged to shift the royal residence from time to time.

Kandy has played an important role in Sri Lankan history, not only as the last capital of Sri Lanka, but also as the last bastion of the Sinhala culture that flourished for more than two thousand years. The long tradition of patronage of traditional values, arts, architecture and literature ended in Kandy with the handing-over of the city by the Sinhala king to the British in 1815. This was the last link in a long continuous chain, but fortunately

Kandy has preserved certain important aspects of the performing arts, architecture and religious practices of the by-gone civilization, providing an opportunity for present and future generations to identify the roots of their past.

A city floating in the heavens

The character of a typical medieval city was preserved when Kandy was established as the capital of the hill country. The hierarchy was emphasized by the privileged location of the royal palace and the temple of the Sacred Tooth Relic high up on the terraces of the eastern hill, overlooking the

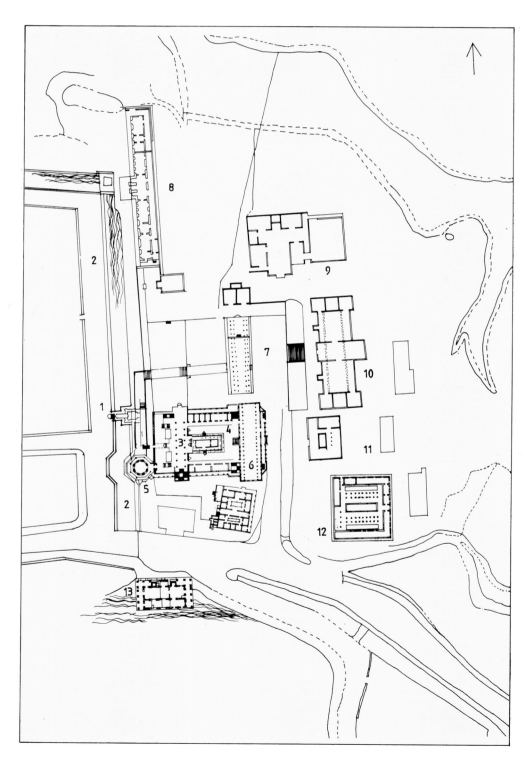

Plan of palace and Tooth Relic temple complex, Kandy
 1. *Entrance*
 2. *Moat*
 3. *Ambulatory*
 4. *Tooth Relic shrine*
 5. *Octagonal library*
 6. *Image house*
 7. *Royal audience hall*
 8. *Sri Vickramarajasingha palace*
 9. *Modern courts complex*
10. *Modern secretariat and courts*
11. *Queen's quarters*
12. *Harem*
13. *Ulpenge or queen's bath*

residential area with its roads laid out on a regular grid orientated to the cardinal points. The palace was physically separated from the sanctuary area by a moat, an open esplanade and a group of religious buildings. The temples dedicated to Natha, Visnu and the Goddess Pattini were planned as sacred precincts surrounded by stone walls with entrance gateways. The temple of the God Kataragama was located within the residential area, but close to the palace.

To the south of the Royal Palace once lay a paddy field, separating it from the Royal Gardens and the Malvatta Monastery complex, until the reign of the last king of Kandy, Sri Vikramarajasimha, who contributed greatly to the improvement and beautification of the city. According to a tradition, the King called for the royal architect, Devendra Mulacariya, and asked him whether he could transform Kandy into a celestial city. This was an extremely difficult task, but the architect asked for time, and after seven days explained his design concept to the King thus, 'Your Majesty, I imagine that the thick green Udawattakele forest behind the palace building is *Nila Megha*, the blue clouds of the sky, and that in front of the palace building it is possible to create cloud-walls in white. Then, by transforming the paddy fields into a lake, one will see the reflection of the cloud-walls and the palace buildings in water, and no doubt it will appear like a city floating in the sky.' The king was very much pleased with the artistic concept of his architect, and in 1810 converted the paddy field into the great lake we see today, thereby adding much to the beauty of the city and giving it its present-day aspect. In keeping with traditional town planning practice, the two monastery complexes, Malvatta Vihara near the royal gardens and the hermitage of Asgiriya Vihara near the royal burial grounds were established for Buddhist monks.

During the 130 years of British occupation of Kandy, the city grew in scale, particularly the residential areas, and many hotels and commercial, residential and administrative buildings were built. In addition many conceptual changes were imposed on Kandy immediately after its occupation by the British who cut down the thick forest surrounding the city for reasons of security, and built three redoubts.

Kandyan art and architecture

The architecture of the Kandyan kingdom cannot be compared either in extent or magnificence with that of the ancient glories of Anuradhapura or Polonnaruwa. Although a continuation of a long-standing tradition that was directly influenced by the buildings of Gampola, Kandyan wooden architecture has a distinct character of its own which responds directly to the needs of a small agricultural community: comfortable rather than luxurious. The buildings are smaller in scale and simpler in appearance, but refined in detailing.

Buildings were mostly of timber and mud on a traditionally moulded, raised stone plinth. Timber doorways, columns, brackets, beams and rafters were intricately carved with traditional decorative patterns. Massive overhanging roofs with long eave projections were double-pitched and covered with flat clay tiles. Lacquer was used in four colours: yellow, red and black with touches of green, in decorating the turned wood columns and balustrades. Door frames and furniture were frequently embellished with finely carved ivory, bone and metal. The refinement of the richly decorated components of Kandyan period architecture give it its distinctive character.

It is possible to trace the development of a well-developed Sinhala painting tradition that originated a few centuries prior to the beginnings of the Christian era. The art of painting has always played an important role in Buddhist architecture as a decorative medium for both facades, and interiors, and the long continuity of the tradition has absorbed the contributions of the many schools which prevailed during different historical periods. The painters of the Kandyan period managed to maintain a distinct identity, while remaining part of an uninterrupted chain of transmission. Kandyan paintings were mostly religious, simpler in composition and decorative in nature, employing a restricted palate, and executed on supports varying from walls, ceilings, doors and windows to furniture, pottery and cloth.

The sculptural works of the Kandyan period were of two kinds. Full relief carving was mainly used for iconographic work. Statues of Buddha and the Hindu pantheon were commonly made out of clay, or of timber with clay plaster, and decorated with metal and ivory or painted with bright colours. Bas-relief, including intricate carvings in ivory, metal, timber and stone, was used in architectural decorations, or to decorate furniture and implements used in day-to-day life.

Buddhism, being a philosophy leading to simplicity in life, did not directly support dancing and music. The dancing and music of the Kandyan period, however, was an integral part of the ritual performances associated with religious ceremonies and processions, as well as agricultural activities. Performances in the King's Court ended with the termination of the royal lineage. Fortunately, the continuity of Kandyan dancing and music has been well preserved as part of a ritual performed at the annual procession, the *Dalada Perahera*, which has been held continuously in honour of the sacred

Palace complex, Kandy.
The Sri Vikramarajasingha palace is seen in the foreground with the octagon of the Tooth Relic shrine and the moat.

Carved timber, Council chamber, Kandy
18th century.
The pillar capitals, the columns and the beams
are exquisitely carved.

Tooth Relic since the fourth century A.D. Today Kandyan dancing is a specialized art form embodying the national identity in the performing arts.

The palace complex

The royal residences, the Temple of the Sacred Tooth Relic, the administrative complex and ancillary buildings, grouped around beautiful court yards, were situated at the eastern corner of the city on terraces along the hill slope, forming a magnificent facade. Originally the palace complex was separated from the rest of the city by a moat, and could be entered only through three doorways. That on the left was the private entrance to the residences. In the centre was the official entrance leading to the council chamber, while to the right was the sacred entrance along the axis of the Temple of the Tooth Relic. The last king of Kandy, Sri Vikramarajasimha, built the present gateway to the palace as a common entrance by joining the official and sacred entrances, in order to provide room for the dominating octagon in front of the palace.

The Tooth Relic

The Sacred Tooth Relic of the Buddha, brought to Sri Lanka during the reign of Kirti Sri Meghavanna (301-328), has been referred to as the palladium of the Sinhala kings. It was protected and venerated by the

161

King, who built a temple for it within the royal palace. Since the reign of Vimaladharmasuriya, the Sacred Tooth Relic has been kept in a specially constructed building, where it has been conserved ever since.

The building which housed the Sacred Tooth Relic of Buddha was always considered an extremely important edifice in Sinhala architecture and was thus located next to the palace. It became a special building type of great importance and was well-decorated and carefully looked after throughout the history of Sri Lanka. Fa-Hsien (399-414 A.D.) states, 'in the city there has been reared also the vihara of Buddha's Tooth, on which, as well as on the other, the seven precious substances have been employed.' Hiuen Tsiang, in 629 A.D., also left a descriptive account of this temple at Anuradhapura and recorded the rituals performed. 'By the side of the king's palace is the vihara of the Buddha's Tooth, several hundred feet high, brilliant with jewels and ornamented with rare gems. Above the vihara is placed an upright pole which is visible night and day from a long distance, and appears like a bright star. Three times a day, the king washes the Tooth of Buddha with perfumed water, sometimes with powdered perfume. Whether for washing or burning, the whole ceremony is attended with a service of the Most Precious Jewel.' As the Temple of the Tooth in Anuradhapura was situated next to the king's palace, the custom continued down to the Kandyan period.

A Portuguese map, perhaps the earliest recorded map of Kandy, dating from the year 1602, shows the general layout of the palace complex during the reign of King Vimaladharmasuriya I. There were two walled squares within the main city, the larger of which could be identified as a residential area, the smaller corresponding to the Nathadevala quadrangle. According to the *Culavamsa*, the Tooth Relic Temple was two-storeyed and built on a picturesque site nearby. The large isolated building drawn above the Natha Devala square may be identified as the Temple of the Tooth built by King Vimaladharmasuriya I. Its true location may be in the present Maha Maluva, between the Natha Devala and the Lake.

Throughout the thirty-one year reign of King Senarath, the successor of Vimaladharmasuriya, there is no record of the building of a temple for the Tooth Relic. This may be due to the political instability experienced during this period; the king left Kandy, and the Tooth Relic was removed to other, more secure, locations. According to the chronicle, 'His son Rajasimha II (1629-87) re-established political stability, ruled in Kandy for fifty-two years, and during this period Rajasimha II built a two-storeyed temple in Kandy to house the Tooth Relic of the Buddha.' No adequate evidence is available to identify or locate this monument.

Vimaladharmasuriya II (1687-1707), 'having attained his consecration as king,...in pious faith in the doctrine of the Victor, prepared in divers ways everything needful for a sacrificial festival for the Tooth Relic. In honor of the Tooth of the Prince of the Wise, he erected a fair three-storeyed *Pasada*, resplendent with all kinds of (artistic) work, and for the sum of five hundred and twenty thousand silver pieces he had a reliquary made, which he covered with gold and ornamented with nine precious stones. In this great reliquary, that resembled a *cetiya* of precious stones, he laid the Tooth of the Victor .

His successor, King Sri Veera Parakrama Narendrasimha (1707-39), 'performed day by day many good works like the giving of alms, and for the rest had books copied, and when he saw that the temple which his royal fathers erected in the capital for the Tooth Relic had fallen into decay, his heart was grieved. The Lord of Men had the beautiful (temple) rebuilt, two-storied, splendid. He provided it with a portal resplendent with all kinds of brilliant ornaments, and...its stucco coating, in colour painting on the two walls of the courtyard. While thus having these thirty-two *jatakas* faultlessly represented in colour painting, the Lord of men laid up an immeasurable store of merit.'

King Narendrasimha did not build a new temple, but he renovated the three-story structure built by his father, and reduced its height to two storeys. In local architectural terminology a 'storey' need not mean a distinct floor. Thus it is possible to visualize a building of two floors with an appearance indicating three storeys. The new roof construcion would have been of a special kind, for the *Culavamsa* specifically mentions that it was 'provided with a graceful roof.'

A plan of the palace complex in Kandy was recorded by Heydt when he accompanied the Dutch Ambassador, Herr Aggreen, in the year 1736. Heydt described the Temple of the Tooth thus; 'to the right is a long and high building, on which were painted all sorts of dragons and foliage in yellow and red colours, and which also is provided with an entrance. When he asked what this was, he was told, through the interpreter, that it was a Pagoda, "in which many Brahmins dwell and make their prayers." All the buildings which I saw there had roofs with coconut leaves or long grass, but the latter is more usual than the former.' There is no doubt that this is a description of the Tooth Relic Temple renovated by King Narendrasimha three years before the end of his reign in 1736.

King Kirtisrirajasimha's reign of thirty-five years (1747-82) corresponds to a Buddhist revival in the Kandyan Kingdom. He built many new temples and renovated most of the shrines that were in decay. This effort was, without any doubt, the most valuable contribution to art and architecture of the Kandyan period. Even though the *Mahavamsa* does not mention that he built a new temple for the Tooth Relic, another chronicle, the *Sulu Rajavaliya,* gives evidence to this contribution. The plan of the palace drawn in 1765, the eighteenth year of his reign, clearly indicated the old shrine and the new Temple of the Tooth. Therefore, it is quite probable that the present Tooth Temple was the work of King Kirtisrirajasimha.

The Kandy palace was not a single edifice, but a complex comprising a large number of small buildings arranged in terraces on a rectangular plan around many open courtyards. Dominating the palace complex from the centre of a vast courtyard was the shrine housing the Sacred Tooth Relic, the principal monument with its own architectural character. Surrounding the courtyard was a series of rooms, also part of the temple complex, which were used for different rituals and other religious and administrative activities. The overall layout is clearly indicated in the 1765 Dutch plan of the Kandy palace complex. The activities connected with the buildings at the entrance and around the courtyard cannot have changed significantly since the time of King Sri Vickramarajasimha, who brought about major

alterations to the complex, and built the octagon (*Pattirippuva*). A descriptive account of the Tooth Relic shrine was given by Hocart as it was in 1931 before it was changed in 1936.

The drumming hall in front of the Tooth Relic shrine was entered from the main doorway to the West, through a beautiful carved stone *Makara Torana* or from the service entrance to the north. The two-storey shrine was physically linked to the drumming hall, leaving an open courtyard around the building on three sides.

Temple of the Tooth Relic, Kandy, 17th-18th centuries.
This is a living shrine with rites and rituals taking place every day. As such the monument itself keeps growing from century to century.

The Tooth Relic shrine

The Tooth Relic Shrine as we see it today is a rectangular building on a magnificent granite base with its long axis running east-west. This stone platform, with its beautifully carved cyma-recta moulding, is a characteristic detail inherited from the Anuradhapura period. It is built of massive and well-dressed granite blocks, fitted neatly together without mortar. The masonry marks clearly carved on the upper surfaces of these slabs, using *Lit Lakunu* (Sinhalese numerals), furnish valuable evidence as to the type of craftsmen and the literary skills of the master builders.

The lower floor is paved with dressed granite slabs and approached from the west, north and south, by means of three flights of steps, the main entrance door being that to the west. Each flight of steps is made up

Carved and painted timber, Temple of the Tooth Relic, Kandy, 17th-18th centuries.
Decorative polychrome timber detailing of the Kandyan school is well represented here.

of four stone blocks with carved risers, and ends in a beautifully carved Kandyan moonstone. They do not, however, have balustrades or guard stones, unlike those found in the early period buildings. A small flight of stairs is also found connecting the drumming hall and the lower floor to the north of the main entrance. These steps are not indicated in the 1765 plan, but would have been added, together with the external staircase leading to the upper floor, at a later date.

The plan of this building is fairly simple, reflecting a long plan prevalent in Sri Lanka. It is a columned structure with a core forming the chamber. The same basic plan is repeated in the upper floor. The palace complex of 1765 gives two identical plans of the old and the new Tooth Relic Shrines. This provides a good example of the tradition of repeating design forms of buildings. In this repetition the dimensions, materials and the details might vary, but the basic form remains unchanged.

Twenty-six granite columns around the verandah support the beams of the upper floor. These pillars are direct descendents of the earlier timber posts which formed the basic architectural style of the Kandyan buildings.

The ground floor is divided into chambers: the elongated front *Digge* and the enclosure to the East, called the *Mahaaramadula*, which corresponds in plan to the Relic Chamber of the upper story. The upper floor is connected directly to the floor above the drumming hall, and the devotees

165

enter the shrine at this level. It has three rooms. The first, where the staircase ends, is the *Handunkudama* or Sandalwood Shed. Two pairs of large elephant tusks have been mounted on decorated stands in this room. The *Handunkudama* has four doors, each timber-framed and inlaid with carved ivory or metal. Those on the west, north and south are entered from the surrounding galleries. That on the east provides access to the ante-chamber in front of the Shrine of Abode, or *Vedahitina Maligava*, which also has painted decorations on all four walls. Directly above the *Mahaaramudala* on the ground floor, this is the chamber containing the Sacred Tooth Relic. It is also known as the *Atulmaligava*.

The Tooth Relic is encased in seven caskets, one kept inside the other, the outermost of which has the shape of a stupa and is adorned with a large number of gold ornaments received as offerings. This casket is placed on a throne decorated with mouldings.

The outer wall of the verandah goes up to the ceiling. It is lime-plastered and whitewashed, the upper part of its outer surface being painted with a decorative frieze of floral motifs. The outer railing of the upper verandah to the north, east and south has turned wooden columns and rails, lacquered in yellow, red and black bands.

Plan and section of Tooth Relic shrine,
Upper floor
1. Ambulatory
2. Entrances
3. Mandapa
4. Antichamber
5. Cella with relic casket
6. Varandah
7. Stairway

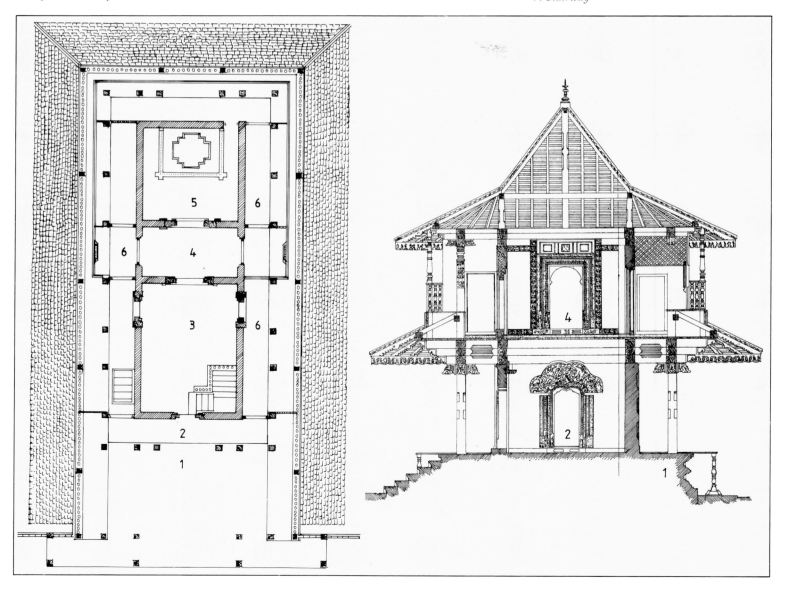

*Decorated timber ceiling, Temple of the Tooth
Relic, Kandy, 17th-18th centuries.
Painted wood is rare and difficult to preserve.*

*Stone doorway, Tooth Relic shrine, Kandy,
17th-18th centuries.
A handsome piece of stone carving.*

Twenty-six timber columns, corresponding to the stone columns at the ground floor level, support the roof structure. The timber columns are beautifully carved with floral patterns and animal motifs, each bearing a four-flowered timber capital or *Pekada* as on the ground floor. A special feature here are the beams supported on columns terminated with a carved bracket and cantilevered away from the building. When more than one beam is placed one on top of the other, the upper beam is always cantilevered more than the lower beam, forming a profile at forty-five degrees. All these beams and brackets were painted with floral, animal and geometric motifs.

As in all traditional Kandy buildings, the roof is the most dominating feature with its cantilevered beams. The roof is in two tiers, the lower being cantilevered out from the first floor, the timber rafters terminating in a metal valance board, a later addition replacing the traditional clay eave-tiles. The upper roof shows the true traditional style with Bo-leaf motifs. The reapers are of the *kitul* palm, and are approximately one centimetre thick by four wide. The roofs have flat clay tiles with horizontal and pointed ends, laid in such a way as to form an interesting pattern.

This building, erected during the reign of Kirtisrirajasimha, followed the traditional architectural expression for a multistorey building which would have existed since the Anuradhapura period. It utilized all art forms that could have been found in a special building of this nature and used materials such as stone, timber, stucco, metal, ivory and terra-cotta. It enshrined nearly all the motifs found in the Sinhala art tradition. This storeyed building would have looked magnificent when it was surrounded by a single-storey structure. Even with the surrounding tall edifice it retains a purity of character worthy of the Sri Lankan tradition.

The Tooth Relic Temple being a very special building in Sinhala architecture, it has become a living museum of the arts. All the inner wall surfaces, ceilings, beams and columns were painted with murals depicting the life of the Buddha, his previous births, and floral and geometrical designs. The stone doorways and moonstones were exquisitely carved and decorated with traditional motifs. The timber doorways were richly inlaid with ivory and metal carvings, and the door sashes with paintings. Terra-cotta was used to decorate the external walls and the roofs. This temple or the inner shrine was not a large building, but a very richly decorated one employing all the materials and media used in Sinhalese art.

The Council Chamber

Popularly known as *Magul Maduva*, the Royal Hall in which the King and his Ministers sat for business of administration and judgement is an excellent example of the timber architecture of the Kandyan period. The present structure was designed by the architect Devendra Mulachariya in 1783 during the reign of King Rajadhi Rajasimhae, and finally completed by Sri Vikrama Rajasimha. Investigations revealed that many additions and changes were carried out during the British occupation. The original hall, measuring 19.75 by 11.65 metres, was later extended towards the north by another 10.33 metres. The present building has 64 beautifully carved timber columns arranged in four rows, two on either side of the centre isle.

Magulmaduva or Council chamber, Kandy, 18th century.
A fine example of Kandyan timber construction with elaborately decorated columns.

Columns ending in carved inverted lotus capitals (*pekada*) supported the dominating timber roof structure with artistically carved beams and rafters forming a hipped roof clad with plain clay tiles. During conservation work, each column was dismantled and steel supports and decayed timber added during the British period were replaced by new timber of the same identified variety. Today this building is used for special national functions presided over by His Excellency the President.

Royal residences and other buildings

The residential palace of the last king was located at the northern end of the building complex. It was a long building with a central doorway leading to an imposing hall decorated with stucco and terra-cotta work. Rooms were disposed in two wings connected by a long verandah facing the inner courtyard. Presently the Museum of the Archaeological Department is housed in this building. The Royal Armoury, the bathing and dressing chamber of the King, the Queen's chambers (*Meda Vasala*) and the harem (*Palle Vasala*) were some of the important buildings which have been preserved intact.

The present High Court building, located on an upper terrace to the east of the Council Chamber, is a two-storey administration building of typical British Colonial architecture dating from 1887. The *Ulpange*, or

169

Queen's bath, was an interesting building situated partly in the lake and partly on land. The original stone-built bathing pool of the queens was later altered by the British, who added another storey using many of the original columns, and converted it into a library, retaining, however, the Kandyan architectural style. The Cultural Triangle, in conserving this building, was faced with many interesting and difficult tasks in removing the ground floor walls while supporting the upper floor and re-exposing the original bathing pool with water.

Other shrines

Natha Devale is the oldest shrine in Kandy, built in the fourteenth century. This stone-built structure, of three-storey expression with a domicile stupa above the inner chamber, is one of the best examples exhibiting South Indian influence. The inner shrine is surrounded by a lofty stone wall bearing an inscription by King Jayavira, and is entered through an open colonnaded hall to the north. It has a beautiful bronze icon of Lokeshvara Natha, a Boddhisatva of the Mahayana Buddhist Pantheon.

Ulpenge - Queen's bath, Kandy, 18th-19th centuries.
Many royal baths exist but this is the only complete example with some modifications carried out during the British period.

Natha devale, Kandy, 17th-18th centuries. The earliest buildings in Kandy are found at the Natha devale complex. Timber and masonry structures were added in later times to the early stone edifice.

The Natha Devale complex was surrounded by a stone moulded boundary wall and entered through a beautifully decorated two-storey roofed archway to the north of the shrine. There were two small stupas of the early periods with image houses, and two Bo-tree shrines located within the boundary wall. Archaeological excavation has revealed the brick remains of an early Bo-tree shrine, and an important fragment of a solid bronze statue of a seated Buddha that would have measured one metre in height.

Maha Devale, the shrine dedicated to the god Visnu of the Hindu Pantheon was found on an upper terrace to the north of the Nathadevale entrance. The shrine was a linear, mud-built structure on a podium, with an upper storey above the sanctuary. It was entered through a two-storey *vahalkada* entrance doorway. Within the temple complex can be seen another small shrine to a local deity and a Bo-tree shrine.

To the west of Nathadevale, across the *Eth Vidiya*, or Elephant Street, was the shrine dedicated to the goddess Pattini. This deity, greatly venerated by the people, was associated with the cure of infections and children's diseases. It was a smaller shrine, with an imposing roof. Before the entrance archway to the shrine at the northern wall was an ancient Bo-tree shrine, its stepped terraced platform affording an imposing view. Another ancient shrine, found to the west of the palace, is dedicated to the god Kataragama or Skanda, whose icon represents a figure with six heads and twelve hands riding on a peacock chariot. A linear building with a two-storey section

above the sanctum, the shrine was entered from the commercial area through a beautiful roofed gateway.

Major monastic complexes

The Buddhist monks in Sri Lanka belonged to three major sects: Siamic, Amarapura and Ramanna. The largest of these, the Siamic sect, was established during the reign of King Kirti Srirajasimha by the Rev. Upali, who brought the higher ordination from Siam, now Thailand. This sect had two chapters, the Malvatta and Asgiriya. Both of these chapters, who had temples scattered throughout the country, have their headquarters located in Kandy.

The Malvathu Mahavihara is located on the south bank of the Kandy Lake. It has many viharas and circuit rooms belonging to the main temples of the Malvatta Chapter. All these residences were grouped around the main chapter house, the *Poyage*, forming beautiful internal courtyards representing traditional architectural forms. The chapter house, located in the central courtyard, was raised on a moulded stone plinth, with a colonnaded verandah on all four sides. The double-pitched hipped roof was covered with plain clay tiles and crowned with two gilded brass pinnacles. The ceiling was decorated with colourful traditional paintings. This sacred building was used for important meetings of the Council, or *sanga-sabha*, and for holding annual higher ordinating rituals.

The Poyamalu Vihara, one of the temples of Malvatta, is located on the same side of the Lake. It has an ancient stupa and an Image House. This two-storey image house has beautiful stone carvings, very probably removed from the previous temple of the Tooth that was dismantled by King Kirtisrirajasinha after completing the present temple. The upper floor of the image house was decorated with paintings, according to the tradition.

Gangarama Vihara is about two kilometres to the east of the palace and near the bank of Mahaweli river. The image house is a very special building built around a ten-metre-high standing statue of the Buddha carved in-situ out of the natural rock. The iconographic style and the facial expressions are representative of the works of the Gampola period. The tall central building is covered with a double-pitched hipped roof of flat clay tiles. Its lower roof, covering the verandah, was built around the main structure. The shrine, entered through a decorated arched door, has its inner walls totally covered with murals drawn during the period of King Kirtisrirajasinha.

The lower part of the walls is decorated with episodes depicting the life of Buddha and his previous births. The upper part of the walls is covered with a large number of paintings of the Buddha. These paintings are of high quality and stylized, showing a different school of Kandyan painting. The drawing of figures and details is exceptionally refined. Investigations have uncovered another inner layer of paintings on the upper part of the wall, probably dating from the Gampola period.

The Hindagala Vihara was part of Malvatta Vihara, but located on the Peradeniya-Galaha road. It was a cave temple on a hill, reached by a long steep flight of stone steps. One of the caves was converted to an image house containing a large reclining Buddha statue. This cave shrine is very important in studying the chronology of Sinhalese paintings, as it enables us to trace the development of Kandyan painting styles over four distinct periods. The earliest paintings, those on the rock ceiling, date from the sixth century A.D. Those inside the cave are from the fourteenth and eighteenth centuries, while the painted decoration of the fafade was done in 1911.

Asgiriya Vihara was the original hermitage monastery of Kandy. Its plan, with the residences built around a central chapter house, is very similar to Malvatta. Vijesunderama Vihara of Asgiriya was architecturally important, and had three special buildings: the old *poyage*, and two image houses with Kandyan period mural decorations.

Adahanamaluva Vihara is situated next to the royal cremation grounds of the Kandyan kings. A stone-built *Gedige* type image house was built

Bodhi tree, Gangarama, Kandy, 18th century. A detail from the paintings at Gangarama vihara.

by King Vikramabahu on the cremation ground of Queen Mother Chandravati. The inner walls of the shrine were decorated with traditional paintings depicting the life of the Buddha and episodes from his previous incarnations.

Mural painting, Ganagarama, 18th century. The linework and decorative details of Kandyan paint work is well expressed in this processional scene.

Kandy today

With the advent of the British, the city of Kandy changed its role and became the service centre of the hill country plantation industry. Three bridges were built, linking the city to Colombo and the other plantation areas. Kandy functioned as the commercial and administrative centre of the Central Province. The city changed its face with the construction of hotels, commercial buildings and churches along the streets in the residential areas of the historic city. Fortunately, the palace complex, shrines and monastic buildings were not drastically changed, but efforts were made to maintain their character and architectural dignity.

The Tooth Temple, one of the most sacred places in the world for Buddhists, is visited by thousands every day. The fascinating and colourful procession, conducted every year in the month of August to venerate the Sacred Tooth Relic, is a tradition unbroken since the fourth century. The most colourful pageant in the country, it is performed for ten days and nights, ending with the full moon, by a thousand drummers and dancers

Painted stone image, Gangarama, 18th century. This polychrome stone image of the Buddha shows how all stone images of the historical period were painted.

in traditional costume marching with nearly a hundred gorgeously caparisoned elephants. This national and religious event gives the city a very special importance in Sri Lanka. Hence the city of Kandy has become a unique city, living in harmony with a beautiful landscape while guarding its cultural and religious importance intact.

The Cultural Triangle

International safeguarding campaign

Roland Silva

The concept of an international campaign on behalf of a cultural heritage project was born in the Nile Valley. The Egyptian Government was about to bury the cultural bones of an earlier civilization for the sake of sustaining another that was yet to be born. Abu Simbel, the treasured monument of Rameses II, was endangered, with its two giant temples carved nearly seventy metres into the natural rock of the cliff on the banks of the stone embankment. The plan of the Egyptian Government was to raise the Aswan dam and collect more water for the people of the country. This, if implemented, would have submerged the two shrines, on the argument that the survival of the present was more important than preserving a dead past.

It was at this juncture that the matter was rightly brought before UNESCO, as the cultural conscience of the world. The debate before the international community was not whether or not Abu Simbel should be allowed to be submerged by the waters of the Nile, but rather whether the present and the past could live together. Therefore, an attempt was made to tap the conscience of the world in order to promote the dual objective of feeding the present while at the same time saving the past.

With this forward-looking decision, the UNESCO machinery was set in motion to mobilize international funding and technical support to save Abu Simbel. The Abu Simbel campaign was the first ripple of a world-wide wave of ideology, and the principles of such a movement had to be clear and acceptable. It was in this context that the 'theme song' of cultural monuments, being not only the product of a people but belonging to the whole of mankind, was sung. Thus, if Abu Simbel and other such edifices belonged to the world, as footprints in the journey of mankind, then the whole of humanity had an obligation to save them for future generations.

The acceptance of Abu Simbel as a project for international assistance and the principle of contributing to save such a monument having been confirmed, the pattern was set for many more safeguarding campaigns. The floods of Venice and Florence in the 1950s that devastated the two principal storehouses of European art treasure elicited immediate support from the international community. Thus the machinery of international campaigns was set in motion, with other sites beyond the Mediterranean being listed: Moenjodaro and Borobudur in Asia were soon identified for international consideration, and it was not long before the nineteenth such campaign was found in Sri Lanka in the 'Cultural Triangle'.

Beginnings

During the centenary celebrations of the Department of Education in 1968, the Archaeological Survey was invited to participate, in view of the fact that a committee had been set up one hundred years previously to consider the potential of Central Government involvement in antiquarianism in Sri Lanka. At the second International Conference on Asian Archaeology held in Colombo in 1969, we prepared a paper entitled 'A Proposal for the layout of the Ancient City of Anuradhapura, Ceylon'. The concluding note stated: 'Although ancient sites such as Villa Adriana near Tivoli, Ostia Antica, the old port of Rome, and Pompei are equally as elaborate as Anuradhapura, these are not as extensive. Hence, a project of this nature, if presented with a suitable planning programme, could easily attract a UNESCO grant for which precedence has already been established.' As a footnote, we referred to an unpublished document of UNESCO by R.Curiel entitled: 'Pakistan: Preservation of historic sites and monuments with a view to cultural tourism'. This was the document that led to the UNESCO Moenjodaro international campaign in Pakistan. We had also acknowledged in this paper the assistance given by R.H. de Silva, Archaeological Commissioner, and K.D.M.C. Bandara, Chairman of the Anuradhapura Preservation Board, as it was at their request that our report was initiated in 1969. Thus, it is clear that the archaeologists in 1969 were aware of the potential of UNESCO campaigns and that Anuradhapura was a suitable site for such an effort.

Not long after this paper was presented, a committee was set up by the then Minister of Education and Cultural Affairs, I.M.R.A. Irriyagolla, to explore the possibility of proposing Ritigala as a site for development under a UNESCO project. The committee was chaired by the Archaeological Commissioner and the author was its Secretary. It was this committee that finally prepared the first Cabinet Memorandum entitled 'The Development of Cultural Tourism in Ceylon (1970)'. The proposed areas of activity included Anuradhapura, Ritigala, Polonnaruva and Sigiriya. The project had an investment tag of Rs. 100 million. The allocation for archaeology was Rs. 55 million and, for hotel and tourist infrastructure, Rs. 45 million. This Cabinet Memorandum, however, was not tabled until the new Government was set up after the elections in 1970.

The new Minister of Cultural Affairs, M.S. Kulatilleke, was not unsympathetic to the concept of UNESCO activity in Sri Lanka. It was during his period of office that we had the visit of G. Bolla, Director of Cultural Heritage, UNESCO, who in 1973 impressed upon the Minister of Cultural Affairs and the Minister of Tourism, P.B.G. Kalugalla that the line of thinking of officials to develop cultural tourism had a high potential and that UNESCO would back Sri Lanka fully on such a programme. G. Bolla also arranged three UNDP projects: a plan for lighting the Dambulla Paintings and the Vatadage area at Polonnaruva, a study of the different stones used in the construction of ancient buildings in Sri Lanka, and the conservation of mural paintings in the country. These projects were all carried out in 1975. At the same time the Cabinet Memorandum covering the Development of Cultural Tourism was revitalized and re-submitted to the Ministers of Cultural Affairs and Tourism. The former signed it but the latter kept it for an extended period and returned it for revision on the basis that it was too long. In the mean time the author was commissioned by UNESCO to write two reports on the potential of Cultural Tourism in Thailand and Bangladesh. This experience added much to the subsequent recasting of the Cabinet Memorandum on the Cultural Triangle for Sri Lanka.

The revised request to the Cabinet of Ministers to develop Cultural Tourism in Sri Lanka was not re-submitted until the second half of 1977. E.L.B. Hurulle, who was extremely keen on this project, spearheaded the local efforts, but once again encountered a set back from tourism. On this occasion the project was submitted entirely as a cultural proposal and the aspect of tourism was less emphasized except as a potential source of income, in order to stress the economic viability of the project.

The year 1978 was an important year for the Cultural Triangle. There was a major UNESCO Educational Conference in Colombo that year, at which the Director-General was present in person, and it was possible to discuss many of the salient features of the Cultural Triangle project. The critical knot to untangle was how the proposal of the campaign could be tabled at the General Conference later in the year. It was here that the wizardry of Ananda Guruge and the author worked. The Minister of Culture and the Secretary for Culture were both busy on the last day of the conference with the question of the return to India of the Kapilavastu relics. It was also the moment for the submission of resolutions at the UNESCO Educational Conference. Ananda Guruge, who was receiving such resolutions on behalf of UNESCO, had received the author in his room for a completely different reason. At the same time, the campaign effort for the Cultural Triangle had reached the floodgates, and it was now a question of how the gates could be opened, and when.

It was the Nepalese delegate to this conference on education that inspired us both to success for he brought in a resolution that the monuments of the Kathmandu Valley be preserved for posterity. After the resolution was accepted the author asked Ananda Guruge what relevance the submission of the Nepalese had on education. In true diplomatic style, he responded that education was, indeed, the mother to many a discipline. The author was prompt on the uptake: 'What about a resolution on the Cultural Triangle?'. 'Yes, why not?', was Ananda's reply, and there we were, turning the key to the door that led to the UNESCO resolution. The Agenda for the UNESCO Eighth General Assembly in 1978 had already been prepared, and the only way for the Cultural Triangle proposal to be tabled was if this resolution drafted then by Ananda stated so, and if the proposal so submitted was accepted at the General Conference on Education that day. Nissanka Wijeratne, the then Minister of Education, was the only person available in the last few minutes to sign such a resolution on behalf of Sri Lanka, and there it was. All the planets were in conjunction and the time was auspicious and right. The Cultural Triangle was on the Agenda of the Eighth General Conference of UNESCO, even without the Cabinet Memorandum covering the subject being approved.

An extraordinary irony of fate was that nearly every proposal submitted concerning the Cultural Triangle failed in its first round. So did the Cabinet Memorandum. Nimalasiri Silva and ourselves went to the Treasury and met the third Silva, Arthur, and asked him exactly what had happened. He was absolutely frank in his comments and admitted that it was he who had advised the Finance Minister to give a negative response to the project in view of the areas of uncertainty which forced the Cabinet to set aside the proposal. However, after an hour-long chat, Arthur was not only convinced, but immediately called for a stenographer for a fresh dictation. It was late for such services, and the author agreed to keep the notes for the new Cabinet Memorandum.

From then on the lights were green all the way up to the UNESCO submission. The fourth Silva, Bandu, played his part as the acting Ambassador and Permanent Delegate to UNESCO. A final back-up from Sri Lanka was considered necessary. Consequently, we prepared a handsome thirty-plate photographic study in black and white, which was hurriedly printed and air-lifted to UNESCO Headquarters. The work at the Paris end was so synchronized that each delegate had a copy of the glossy photographic study when the vote was called for the Cultural Triangle. The well-prepared presentation was so convincing that no one could ever have opposed it.

UNESCO in turn played its part. S.J. Stultz, the new Director of Cultural Heritage, was in Sri Lanka by March 1979 to prepare the work-plan and the protocol for signature. This was presented to UNESCO's Executive Board by August, and approval was obtained for a campaign inauguration. The then Prime Minister of Sri Lanka, Hon. Ranasinghe Premadasa, in keeping with the Cabinet Paper, assumed his role as the chairman of the special committee to guide the destinies of the Cultural Triangle. This committee continued to meet on a monthly basis for nearly a year and a half until the Board of Governors of the newly created Central Cultural Fund became the successors to this special committee in December 1980, long after the two inaugurations of the Cultural Triangle. Two other important events took place in 1979: the collection of money which began in March with the introduction of an all-inclusive 'tourist ticket' of US$ 10 to cover admittance to the main sites, and the preparation of the UNESCO documentary film on the Triangle in August. It is this film that convinced the member states to support the Cultural Triangle campaign so generously.

The launching of the international campaign

The dawn of the 1980s was most auspicious for the Cultural Triangle. The first of January 1980 was a full-moon day and one of the most auspicious days of the year. Every effort was made to convince the Director-General of UNESCO to be present in Sri Lanka on that day to inaugurate the campaign. Sri Lanka stood firmly by this date and caused a semi-miracle to take place. We had hardly two months to prepare what was to be one of the most spectacular inaugurations of the century. We all thought and acted big, following the guidelines of the chairman of this committee, the Prime Minister.

We said to ourselves that there were 3,000 monks at Jetavana monastery in its hey-day and that for the inauguration of its restoration we must have an equal number; 3,000 chairs were provided and we had 4,000 participants. We asked for 10,000 children dressed in white to sit on the stone paving of the upper terrace; this too was done. The full complement of the Cabinet of Ministers was to be present on the inauguration dais. We hoped that 100,000 persons would attend and there were double the number on the occasion. The operational strategy was simple: we wrote to each of the 160 Members of Parliament to send 1,000 participants from each electorate, and there were 40,000 in excess. In the same way we had asked for 20 monks from each electorate and there were 1,000 in excess. There was a full turnout of ambassadors, and each had to plant a tree in the 'diplomatic garden' set up to the south of the stupa, which is now shady and green.

The vast upper terrace of the stupa was decorated along its perimeter with two hundred flag poles and a drummer to each pole. Strands of bunting in the colours of the Buddhist flag were draped from the top of the giant stupa to the base of each flag pole. The colour and spectacle of the occasion was completed by the procession of dignitaries, accompanied by dancers and drummers, who circumambulated the stupa once before climbing to the top of the three basal terraces and placing there a relic-casket to the chanting of sacred verses by the Buddhist monks. In their speeches the orators related the history of the site. It was then that the Chairman and the Prime Minister inaugurated the 'One Rupee Campaign' requesting the young and old to contribute one rupee every year for ten years, thereby raising the 150 million rupees required for the conservation of this Buddhist stupa, the tallest in the world. With this announcement, one thousand boy scouts radiated out from the base of the stupa, each with a collection box in hand. Among the dignitaries present were the high priest of the Bo-tree temple, the representative of the Director-General of UNESCO, M. Makagiansar, the Prime Minister, and the President of Sri Lanka.

The formal inauguration of the work of the Cultural Triangle subsequently took place at the Historic Audience Hall of Kandy, on the morning of the full moon of August 1980. The guests included the Venerable *Mahanayakas* of the various Chapters, the heads of the other religions, the President of Sri Lanka, the Prime Minister, the Director-General of UNESCO, all the members of the Cabinet and the full Diplomatic corps. During the day the Director-General of UNESCO visited the religious dignitaries and viewed the UNESCO film. The climax to the inauguration was a performance of the age-old Tooth Relic procession that has been enacted year in year out since the fourth century A.D. This spectacle of a hundred decorated elephants, a thousand dancers and an equal number of drummers is a sight unrivalled in any other part of the world.

In order to implement the work of the Cultural Triangle efficiently and to be able to initiate further projects of this nature, a new, autonomous management structure had to be created. The 'Central Cultural Fund' was established by an Act of Parliament in order to provide for the administrative functioning of the project   and the management of its resources. Various inducements and benefits were proposed in the Bill in order to encourage contributions, as well as reduced burdens of duties and taxes on the Fund and various safeguards. With the passing of this Act on 17 December 1980, the extempore special committee of management was absorbed into the Board of Governors of the Central Cultural Fund. The Prime Minister was the Chairman of this new Board and the Ministers in charge of Cultural

Affairs, Finance, Tourism, UNESCO Matters and Hindu Affairs were all ex-officio members. The financial concessions were the maximum that the Bill could provide, equalled only by the President's Fund. The scope of work envisaged under the Act does not restrict activities to mere archaeology but has the broadest interpretation of culture.

Criteria for selection of projects

In the selection of projects for the Cultural Triangle, we tried at first to follow the UNESCO precedent, but the attempt failed as all of the previous international safeguarding campaigns had involved only a single monument, or at best a single site, such as the stupa of Borobudur or the ancient city of Moenjodaro. Mr Stultz and the Sri Lankan team had little alternative but to break new ground in Sri Lanka by widening the scope and concept of a UNESCO campaign. Having visited Anuradhapura, Polonnaruva, Sigiriya, Dambulla and Kandy, it was difficult to leave out any of them, as each was of universal cultural and historical significance, and was of potential interest to the international community. It is, indeed, for these reasons that all of the projects nominated for the Cultural Triangle are today World Heritage Sites.

In order to justify the scope of the campaign to UNESCO's Executive Board, it was considered prudent to identify those outstanding features in each site which would merit its being the subject of a UNESCO campaign. Let us, then, briefly examine the reasons that compelled us to identify and propose, for adoption by the international community, six sites concerning the preservation of ancient monuments and one cultural heritage project for preserving a living tradition.

Abhayagiri Monastery

Abhayagiri Monastery is one of seventeen such religious units in Anuradhapura and the largest of the five major viharas of this city. Founded in the second century B.C., it had grown into an internatinal institution by the first century of this era, attracting scholars from all over the world and encompassing all shades of Buddhist philosophy. The liberal nature of the institution made it possible for both Theravada and Mahayana concepts to grow side by side. The influence of Abhayagiri Vihara extended to the source of Buddhism in Bodh Gaya and also to the centre of Mahayanism in Nagarjunakonda in the Deccan. The introduction of Buddhism to China promoted pilgrim traffic, and learned monks visited Sri Lanka and carried away to those far-away lands the Sacred Texts and the precepts of religion as they were practised here. The sea traffic had its impact on the ports of call, and soon Java, Thailand and Burma had branch monasteries of Abhayagiri around the eighth century. The centre-piece of this monastery is a stupa of majestic proportions reaching to a height of approximately 112 metres.

The reason that UNESCO selected this monastery for the campaign effort was the striking fact that Abhayagiri was one of the largest pilgrim establishments ever built by man, and that was as early as the fifth century A.D. It was not until the thirteenth century A.D., that even the great Christian monasteries of France such as Cluny, the mother-house of the

Benedictines, could count 5,000 monks. The area of the Abhayagiri monastery covers over 200 hectares and has substantial edifices to house this number. The administrative procedures, teaching methods and religious disciplines followed at this institution can well be recreated from the buried remains at the site. In fact, such data can prove to be a revelation to monastic organization and even an example for present-day university life.

Jetavana Monastery

The reason for the selection of Jetavana was entirely due to the magnitude of the stupa which at over 120 metres in height is the tallest stupa in the world and indeed the tallest brick building ever completed by man. The religious symbolism and technical achievements of this edifice are of international appeal and a study fascinating to man.

The dome is indeed a very special design. Its shape has evolved, in our opinion, to a perfect mathematical equation which if extended to its logical mirror image forms a perfect spheroid comparable to those of the universe. It can also be proved that this product of bricks and clay mortar and its various angles of repose are all a by-product of many centuries of experimentation with full-scale construction; a design product of inductive logic or an outcome of the tests of time through 'trial and error'. The brilliant design of the architects of old was developed gradually, culminating in the great stupa of the Jetavana which stands even today as a towering monument to the masters of brick-masonry.

The Jetavana stupa is the tallest Buddhist monument in the world and is still from the point of view of brick technology, the tallest edifice constructed of this material in the world. Therefore, both from a religious and a technological point of view, the Jetavana stupa qualifies as an outstanding monument of mankind.

Alahana Parivena

Polonnaruva was a military stronghold before it became the capital from the tenth century A.D., to the thirteenth century. The city was occupied in the tenth century by invaders from the South of India, the Colas. At least fourteen Hindu shrines bear witness to the growing influence of Southern India at that time. It was in the twelfth and thirteenth centuries that Polonnaruva experienced its golden age under one of the most illustrious kings of Sinhala history, Parakramabahu the Great. By constructing immense lake reservoirs and irrigation canals, this sovereign gave prosperity to his kingdom.

He also founded in the twelfth century Alahana Parivena, a great monastic complex which is situated North of the outer city wall. The monastery consists of two big stupas, the Rankotvehera and the Kirivehera, the largest image house, Lankatilaka, the great chapter house and numerous dwelling cells built on several terraces. Excavations also revealed the existence of other important edifices, a hospital, a chapter house, alms hall and ponds. The UNESCO and Sri Lankan teams working out the selection list for the joint work programme had thus to pay due consideration to the establishment concept of the Alahana Parivena on the basis of a flourishing teaching institution or university working at full capacity during the twelfth century A.D., After the thirteenth century, Polonnaruva also suffered the fate of Anuradhapura and was covered by the jungle for over six hundred years.

Among the most exceptional monuments conserved at Polonnaruva is the unrivalled group of four sculptures that have been cut out of the living rock at the Galvihara. The largest of these recumbent figures is an exquisite piece of sculpture apart from being a revered image and much worshipped. The standing statue of the Buddha with the unusual hand posture of *Anamisalochana* is a masterpiece of expression and a subject of deep meditation. The two others in a seated posture are of exquisite workmanship and form a group with the rest that together constitute an internationally accepted unit of cultural property of the highest ranking.

Sigiriya Rock Fortress, Boulder and Water Gardens

The uniqueness and universal significance of this site were immediately apparent. Sigiriya has to be appreciated on many counts. It is unique as a work of town planning. It is well known for its gardens which are of three types, water, boulder and terrace. A good millennium older than the Italian gardens of the Renaissance and the Moghul water gardens, dating from the fifth century A.D., the Sigiriya gardens rank among the earliest extant landscaped gardens. The paintings on the rock-face are classed with the finest in the world. The literature scribbled on the mirror wall with a collection of one thousand six hundred poems is a cultural treasure which is, indeed, the finest in the Sinhala language.

As a city it is already declared as a treasure on the World Heritage List. Even before its selection by man, nature had carved in its features the excellence that it still portrays, a boulder of giant proportions perched like a 120-metre diameter mass sitting on smaller rocks with the summit elevated 180 metres above the plain. The four acres of ground of the palace complex on the summit survey the horizon on all sides. The terrace, boulder and water gardens cascade down to the west with the colours of the sunset mirrored against the reflecting waters. The unexcavated city to the east has many a hidden thought for conjecture. Is it the civil administration? Was it for the citizens? Or was it yet another extension of the palace compound? These will all be answered once the archaeologists place their spades in it. The two religious institutions were to the north and the south-west. The unauthenticated view of the remains on the southern ridge were for the abodes of the ministers of state.

The many-faceted site of Sigiriya which has such a wide array of cultural selection can potentially be a high attraction among quality visitors. In any event the drama and spectacle of the landscape is such that the interest of all visitors at Sigiri can be sustained. The fact of Sigiri being a successful candidate for selection under the Cultural Triangle Project was never in doubt.

The painted caves at Dambulla

Dambulla accounts for the largest collection of ancient mural paintings on one site. Sri Lanka is rich in this regard although the bulk of the paintings are from the eighteenth and nineteenth centuries. The five caves on the southern escapement of the rock have 2,000 square metres of classical murals. It is for this reason that Dambulla has been included in the Cultural Triangle programme.

The earliest remains of paintings in Sri Lanka may be dated to about the second century A.D., in sites such as Vessagiri in Anuradhapura and later at Kotiyagala, to the south of the island. Sigiriya in the fifth century comes fairly high in terms of its chronology, which suggests that there must have been a well-established school of painters prior to this period. With the high watermark of Sigiri paintings we see an element of baroque intrusion in the details of Hindagala dated to the eighth century and those at Puligoda and Mahiyangana which precede the twelfth-century efforts at the Tivamka Pilimage. After this period the paintings are rare, with occasional appearances as seen at the upper chamber of Gadaladeniya, until the Kirti Srirajasimha period. It is quite possible that many temples were over-painted during this phase as seen even at Dambulla. However, our largest resource of murals come from the eighteenth-century period and of these Dambulla is the finest. There are well over 500 temples with paintings in this country and this is a treasure that is most delicate and must be preserved for posterity.

Kandy: a living City

Kandy, the last capital of Sri Lanka, still retains the vestiges of the rites and rituals of the lost kingdoms of the Sri Lankan people. Although Colombo has been the political capital for nearly 175 years, the religious and cultural capital of this country continues to be Kandy. Therefore, although the palace is unused, the other associated establishments all perform their part as it was before the British occupied it. The Sacred Temple of the Tooth still remains the most revered place in Sri Lanka with the presence of a bodily relic. The Nathadevalaya, where the anointing of kings took place, is still an active place with a religious shrine dedicated to the deity. There are objects of Buddhist worship as well, such as the stupa, Bo-tree and image house. The Visnu Devale stands nearby and has been a flourishing shrine since it was originally brought from Aluthnuvara. This also has a Bo-tree shrine. Pattini Devala is the other shrine which again is part of the sacred edifices of the core city.

Beyond the immediate centre are the two major monasteries of the two Venerable Mahanayakes; one across the southern lake at Malvatta and the other to the north on Asgiri hill. A few other outstanding shrines on the periphery of the city are Hindagala, Suduhumpola, Gangarama and Vijayarama. The value of this sacred city is in the collective activities of all these institutions, be they ritual, custom or rites. These activities reach a climax during the full moon of August when all the aged and the young, the intellectuals and the simple-minded, rich and poor meet to pay homage to the Sacred Tooth taken out along the streets in procession. This custom of an annual procession has been carried out year in year out since the fourth century A.D., when the Tooth Relic was brought to Sri Lanka. Fa-hsien the Chinese Pilgrim who stayed at Abhayagiri for two years in 412 and 413 A.D., discusses this ritual in great detail and as it took place in Anuradhapura.

It is this environmental synthesis of man and nature with the performing and plastic arts, the ritual and ceremonies and the history and age-old traditions which continue to be an integral part of the life of the people as seen in Kandy that led to its inclusion in the Cultural Triangle programme.

Restoration work will clear away many of the modern accretions, while preserving the surrounding natural features of the lake and forest and retaining the charm of the old trading areas where people have continued to live amidst the town houses of the old governors or *disavas* of Kandy. The work includes the excavation of the earliest remains and conserving the finds, acquiring the buildings that have lost their ritual functions and restoring their original attributes, laying out the inner city to its original and pristine glory, conserving the shrines that are relevant to religious and cultural upliftment, controlling the inroad of tradespeople and industrialists into the inner city and the religious areas and providing the right atmosphere for religious and cultural activities to flourish.

Cultural complex: Colombo

The purpose of a new Cultural Complex for Colombo was to provide for the living traditions of art and culture. At the same time there were major activities in which the Culture Ministry was engaged such as the translation of old texts and preparation of dictionaries and encyclopaedias. There were also many societies covering the various arts of the country and these had to be provided with sustenance and support. All in all there was no place in Colombo or elsewhere which could be called a centre for culture and where one could be exposed to all these facets of the Sri Lankan cultural scene. Such a centre would also introduce foreign visitors, not only to the sites of the Triangle, but also to the many historic sites through scale models of the ancient cities outside Colombo.

With these objectives in view it was thought appropriate to identify an area of Colombo which had already been groomed to such attractions. Thus a plot of around 15 hectares of land surrounding the Colombo Museum, the Art Gallery and the John de Silva Theatre was selected as a suitable site. Apart from the three institutions mentioned, which would remain as the nucleus of the complex, the rest of the area was to be developed to house the existing governmental and non-governmental institutions allied to the Ministry of Culture and other cultural organizations and activities. A positive effort was to be made to attract the private institutions that had already been established to foster the different arts, such as drama, dance, painting, sculpture, music, theatre or film, or literature. Even associations of professional bodies such as those of archaeologists, numismatists, lyricists, architects, historians and linguists could be encouraged to meet in these congenial surroundings and so create the atmosphere of a true cultural centre.

These were the objectives that surrounded the establishment of the Cultural Complex of Colombo. At the same time the essentials for such activity would be the need for theatres, exhibition halls, lecture halls and rooms for listening to music or projecting films. Restaurant services and craft shops could also contribute to cultural aspirations. Finally, the

Cultural complex Colombo.
A centre to provide for the living traditions of art and culture reflecting a national trait that could be called Sri Lankan. (overleaf)

185

architecture of such a complex should, in many ways, reflect a national trait that could be called Sri Lankan.

Administration

In order to implement the Cultural Triangle campaign in Sri Lanka, the Central Cultural Fund Act No.57 of 1980 was enacted. It was the first time in Sri Lanka that we have had a Prime Minister as Chairman of a Corporation, and that the Board of Governors includes the Ministers of Culture, Finance, UNESCO Matters, Tourism and Hindu Affairs, as well as the Deputy Minister of Culture, the Commisioner of Archaeology, the secretaries to the Prime Minister and the Minister for Cultural Affairs, and two personalities apppointed directly by the Prime Minister, and emphasizes the importance the Government attaches to this project.

The Board of Governors meets once every month and decides on the general policy with a view to implementing the work plan prepared jointly by UNESCO and Sri Lanka and signed on 25 August 1980 at the inauguration. In order to monitor the implementation of this plan in accordance with the work programme and time schedules, a Working Group consisting of a team from UNESCO and a team appointed by the Board of Governors meets every year and publishes its findings. With a view to assisting the Board of Governors on a continuing basis a Staff, Policy and Establishments Committee has been appointed with the Secretary to the Prime Minister as its Chairman and representatives of the Treasury, Public Administration and the Ministries associated with the Central Cultural Fund and the Director-General.

The items of work to be implemented have been listed under seven major projects. In order that these projects may be implemented with proper co-ordination, seven honorary Steering Committees have been setup. Together with these, there is also a Steering Committee of academics for the laboratories, another for publicity and yet another for finance. The Board of Governors initially selects the Chairman of each Steering Committee and, thereafter, the Chairman handpicks his team according to the guidelines set out. It has been suggested that each team retain the following professionals if the Chairman is not one of them: (a) lawyer; (b) accountant; (c) architect/engineer/senior contractor; (d) travel personality; and (e) mediaperson.

At an *ex-officio* level the following are also included: (a) the religious head of the shrine; (b) chief administrative officer; (c) director-general; (d) archaeological director; (e) conservation director; and (f) assistant director development (co-ordinator).

These committees meet about once every two months and visit the sites at least twice each year. The subjects discussed at each meeting are generally on the basis of a report on: (a) excavation; (b) conservation, and (c) administration and finance. Reports of these meetings are always tabled before the Board of Governors.

Day to day implementation of the projects is through archaeologists, architectural conservators and administrative and financial personnel. The staff members of these teams meet twice every month on a given day and attend to the different disciplines of the project. Meetings are held

alternately on site and in Colombo. The site meetings concentrate on the master plan of work for the year and monitoring progress. Those held in Colombo concentrate on administrative and financial matters. The minutes of these meetings must be circulated within 48 hours so that the work discussed can be implemented according to the conclusions. Decisions taken at these meetings cannot be altered except at another progress meeting and so the collective and democratic conclusions are all upheld, be it on administrative, financial or scientific matters. We believe that the success of the work of the Cultural Triangle has been due to this democratic process, where decisions on implementation are arrived at only after adequate discussion. For these reasons it is critical that attendance at the meetings is strict; anyone absent without valid reason remains on leave until the matter is settled.

The actual work programme on each project is implemented by the two scientific directors covering archaeology and architectural conservation. They have a number of assistant directors and there is a chief supervisor and other technical officers. The skilled and unskilled labour work under such supervisors whether for excavation or conservation activities. Administration in the field is carried out by a project manager who is either an architect conservator or an archaeologist. The work quantum is controlled on the basis of both quality and quantity and there are work norms for the daily input. Any deviation from this appears in the monthly bar charts of performance and the supervisors have to answer for any variation.

Finance

The funding of the Triangle campaign had to be suitably negotiated so that there was a fair share of participation by Sri Lanka as well as by the international community. At the very inception, in fact on the day after the inauguration, 26 August 1980, the Minister of Cultural Affairs proposed to the Director-General of UNESCO that Sri Lanka should contribute 40 per cent which UNESCO would be requested to provide the remaining 60 per cent. This ratio has been a type of gentleman's agreement throughout. The total funding was to be generated from national and international sources, based on the following lines on an approximate calculation as revised up to 1991:

National Funding

Government contribution	Rs.	450,000,000
Tourist receipts	Rs.	500,000,000
Public contribution	Rs.	30,000,000
Miscellaneous collections	Rs.	20,000,000
Total	**Rs.**	**1,000,000,000**

Foreign Funding

WFP	Rs.	380,000,000
UNDP	Rs.	50,000,000
UNESCO	Rs.	25,000,000
Member States of UNESCO	Rs.	650,000,000

Miscellaneous	Rs.	95,000,000
Total	**Rs. 1,200,000,000**	

This gives a rounded sum of Rs. 2,200 million, which matches the total cost estimate of Rs.2,177 million. The expenditure up to the 1990s was Rs. 424 million and therefore a balance of Rs. 1,753 million will have to be met in the next few years if the project is to be concluded, at least by 1996. The tourist collection, at Rs. 165 million by the end of 1990, flagged after 1983 with the troubles, but picked up again by 1989 and hopefully will move on to better times to reach the balance of Rs. 335 million. Public contributions have been pretty low and this will be stimulated in the next three years to reach the Rs. 30 million mark. The target of collections has focussed on the sale of books, performances given by various countries and contributions such as the medals donated by the former USSR, all of which have combined to build up good will and add much-needed resources to the Fund.

In terms of the UNESCO effort to encourage foreign funding, the biggest contribution has been from the World Food Programme, which has a committed Rs. 380 million provision or the cost of 4,800 labourers per day for a fifteen-year period. This has been contributed in the form of food by the WFP. UNDP has made a donation to the laboratories of the Cultural Triangle in two instalments. First, U.S.$ 300,000 under the second country programme, and U.S.$ 700,000 under the fourth country programme. UNESCO itself seldom contributes, but has provided vital seed money to get the project moving.

The United Kigdom came at a critical phase of funding when tourism had dropped to its lowest ebb and the Cultural Triangle programme would have been closed if not for its timely assistance, but it was Japan that really got the whole project started with the first investment and this was repeated four times in varying amounts in the form of transport, equipment and machinery. The Chinese contribution to the two stupas provided the finale to the funding effort and the crowning of these two tallest stupas in the world will be an appropriate ceremony to the conclusion of the largest UNESCO Heritage Project ever implemented. Several million rupees have been received and more are expected from other likely donor countries in the form of ad hoc contributions such as scholarships, equipment, publicity, experts and so forth.

One of the novel innovations by the Cultural Triangle for funding purposes was the build-up of public opinion in donor countries by forming 'Charity Companies'. These institutions were incorporated under the Companies Act, their shareholders being friends of Sri Lanka. Such organizations plead on behalf of Sri Lanka for the heritage of this country with a view to safeguarding the cultural property of mankind. They have provided expertise, equipment and funds, but above all campaign within their respective governments to assist the Cultural Triangle project. Such Charity Companies exist in Australia, France, Germany, Japan, Singapore, Benelux, the Scandinavian regions and the United Kingdom.

Scientific aspects

The scientific aspects of the two disciplines of Excavation and Conservation

commenced on a firm base. First of all the personnel were selected from among the best in the land. Every opportunity was provided for external specialists to work with Sri Lankan colleagues and thereby extend a friendly hand in the gigantic task of excavating and conserving the most extensive area ever undertaken in a single project in this country. The Directors of Archaeology and the Directors of Conservation had to take some important decisions before any work began at the sites. These consisted of the following:

1. All aspects of prospecting were to be carried out before any excavations began. These included the following:

   (a) Contour surveys were made of all the sites at half-metre intervals. These also included a 30-metre grid planned on a north-south, east-west orientation. Concrete pegs were placed with level nails positioned on each. The ruins visible on the surface were all plotted. So were the buildings, roads and other man-made features. Natural objects such as trees were all marked with indications of their heights.

   (b) Aerial photographs were taken of all the sites at the lowest altitude of flying ever carried out in Sri Lanka, i.e. 1,500 metres.

   (c) A resistivity survey was begun but without much success. The initial studies by Prof. Hess of Paris proved the exercise to be widely out and, although a substantial portion of Jetavana was attempted, it was later abandoned.

2. Various aspects of documentation were formulated including the traditional and the innovative.

   (a) Keeping to the traditional, it was agreed that the grid system will be followed using 81 pits to a 30-metre square. It was also agreed that we would excavate at least one of the 81 pits down to virgin soil. The rest would be excavated to the level of the last important cultural phase. The measurement methods in terms of levels and horizontal dimensions were agreed upon. The types of data concerning special finds, pottery, soils, building remains and stratifications were all to be noted in a standard science book.

   (b) The thought that every site once excavated is destroyed forever pressed us to devise the most advanced recording system ever applied in field archaeology so far in any part of the world. This is the technique of vertical photogrammetry which is applied to every stratificated level in an excavation pit. Such three-dimensional photography will enable every stratum to be re-examined under stereoscopic study even in a hundred years with magnification of a high order. Thus the very archaeologists working at these sites will give themselves a second opportunity to question their own theories at a later date or even provide their critics a sporting chance to formulate parallel alternatives.

   (c) The acceptance of the computer data bank by the Cultural Triangle project imposed a further discipline on the numerous archaeological directors. This meant a series of mutual dialogues among the specialists to discuss and come to terms concerning

certain data recording systems covering the special finds, pottery and the context cards of the stratified layers.

3. The traditional methods of the analysis of finds was combined with newer methods of dating. After all, the important precept in archaeology was to be able to date a stratum and, thereby, the finds from each level. In this regard we have introduced in a big way the techniques that are most useful for historical excavations.

   (a) The technique of thermoluminescence is the method by which the silica particles of any burnt object can be analysed and the date of the last burning observed. Hence a brick, tile, pot, etc., could all be dated in terms of the day of firing the brick or tile or the last day of use of a pot for heating or cooking.

   (b) Carbon 14 is a slightly older technique which we are using in the Cultural Triangle, but without the use of our own equipment. However, the technique is expensive so that sampling is selective

4. The publication of excavation reports has been imposed on the directors of archaeology as a firm disicipline. It was agreed at the start that excavation material will be published as field records and not as comparisons in the first instance. The comparison stage will be left to their old age, or to other archaeologists throughout the world who might be invited to handle this aspect of the work.

5. The excavated special finds and the pottery, once analysed, checked and treated, will be deposited in a site museum built for the purpose at each venue. The excavation records will also be kept there, but for purposes of safety and in order to ensure a second record, excavation field books will be duplicated and one copy kept in the National Archives. There will be a mini-laboratory attached to each of the site museums to carry out this work.

6. The architectural material unearthed by excavation or exposed by conservation will all be recorded in the first instance as a preliminary survey report. Thereafter some decisions have to be taken as to conservation strategy. The treatment methods have to be discussed and if they are different to the standard techniques, then they have to be submitted to the Statutory Advisory Board, of the Department of Archaeology. With the approval of the Advisory Board, the work will then be carried out by the conservation staff with proper supervision of quality and quantity. The Architectural Firms have to certify for such standards before payments are made at the end of each month. They also have to prepare an annual report of conservation done each year.

7. Once the monuments are conserved, the site needs to be well laid out and the amount of flora and fauna considered. Other features of sites for the services of pilgrims and visitors have to be worked out. Most of these sites have some monks and a modern temple. This has to be harmoniously integrated into the area of modern buildings including the museum and the car park. Visitor facilities include a sales centre, a model of the site and essential services such as sanitary and refreshment facilities, signposting, maps and

guidebooks, taped descriptions, slides and even floodlighting. Roads, visitors' trails and footpaths are essential, and some garden furniture will also be needed.

Future

The future of these sites will have to be considered from two points of view: firstly, as religious sites with monks and pilgrims playing their part as a religious establishment, and, secondly, visitors should be able to enjoy the cultural heritage of mankind in terms of art, sculpture and architecture. At the same time these sites can generate substantial resources, which the service elements for such visitors require order and regulated practice. Thus a whole line-up of management services with a profit component can well be visualized. In fact, the profit component could be substantial to the extent that if the profits are properly diverted, other projects of this nature can also be implemented, the exercise continued and the process made self-generating.

Glossary

ankusa
A goad used by elephant keepers to control elephants. One of the eight auspicious symbols.

Anotaptavila
A mythological lake in the Himalayas.

apsara
A celestial nymph.

arhat
An enlightened disciple of the Buddha.

asanaghara
A shelter for a sacred throne such as a vagirarana, which is a replica of the traditional stone seat upon which the Buddha attained enlightenment.

astamangala
The right auspicious symbols of Buddhism.

ayaka
The Altar-like projections of the lowermost basal terrace surrounding a stupa, and facing the four cardinal points.

bhadripita
One of the eight auspicious symbols.

bhikkhu
Buddhist monk.

bhikkhuni
Buddhist nun.

bodhighara
A shrine in which the principal object of worship is a sacred Bodhi-tree.

bodhisattva
A Buddha-to-be, or the historical Buddha in previous lives.

brahmin
A member of the priestly caste of the Hindu Indian social system.

Buddha charita
The life-story of the historical Buddha, Siddharta Gautama.

caitya or cetiya
An object of worship, often used to signify either a Buddhist relic-monument or a stupa.

char bagh, or chahar bagh
A Persian and later Urdu term meaning 'four gardens'.

carmara
Flywhisk: one of the eight auspicious symbols.

chatra
Umbrella.

chattravati
A series of umbrellas stylized to form the conical part of the superstructure of a stupa.

cittasala
Belvedere.

culavamsa
The second part of the *Mahavamsa,* or Great Chronicle.

dagaba
See stupa.

danasala
Refectory for monks.

devale
A shrine to a deva, a god.

devalakotuva
The cylindrical portion of the superstructure of a stupa corresponding to the stem of the chattravati.

dhamma
Buddhist canonical law or precept.

digge
An ante-chamber beyond the mandapa or vestibule in a devela.

drip-ledge
The man-made capillary channel cut into the overhang of a rock shelter in order to protect it from rain-water.

garbha
The domical section of a stupa, or the sanctum of an image-house.

gedige
A domical stone or brick building.

giri
A hill or mount.

giri durga
'Mountain barrier', i.e., a hill fortress.

guardstone
The vertical stupa for the coping-stone of the sloping balustrade which has now been stylized to form part of an ornamental classical entrance.

hastivedi
A retaining wall ornamented with elephants facing forwards.

hataraskotuva
The cubic superstructure of a stupa, whose sides are stylized to resemble a wooden or stone fence.

inselberg
A large, mountainous mass of rock formed by the erosion of early geological strata.

Jain
A follower of Jainism.

Jataka
'Birth Stories'. An extensive collection of traditional Buddhist tales concerning the previous incarnations of the Boddhisattva, or Buddha-to-be.

jala durga
'Water barrier', i.e., a moat.

kandavurunuvara
Fortified town.

katakamudra
Pinnacle of a stupa or of a peaked building.

kota
Pinnacle of a stupa or of a peaked building.

kotkaralla
The conical part of the superstructure of a stupa.

magulmaduva
Audience hall of the king.

makara
A mythical, composite aquatic monster, symbolically associated with Time and Water.

makara torana
An arch formed by the bodies and tails of two makaras.

mandapa
Open front hall of a building or open building.

mara paraja
The defeat of Mara the God of Evil and overcoming the temptation.

meghalata
'Cloud maidens', or personifications of the clouds.

moonstone
The frontal semi-circular first step of the entrance to most ancient buildings in Sri Lankan classical architecture.

mula
A faculty or administrative division of an old Buddhist monastery.

nagaraja
Anthropomorphic Cobra-King.

oya
A seasonal river.

pansala
Buddhist temple or monastery.

pancavasa
Five-unit residential and teaching complex.

panka durga
A 'mud barrier', i.e., a swamp or mud-moat.

parinibbana, or parinirvana
The ultimate state of non-being in the chain of re-birth.

pasada, or prasada
Architecturally a multi-storeyed stepped structure.

patimaghara
Buddhist image-house

Pattra tree
The bo-tree under which Gautama Buddha attained enlightenment.

pekada
The capital of a column.

perahara
Religious or social procession.

pesavalahi
The circular steps at the base of a stupa between the dome and the terrace.

pilimage
Buddhist image-house.

poyage
The chapter house of a Buddhist monastery.

prasada
See pasada.

punkalasa, or purnaghata
Pot of plenty, one of the eight auspicious symbols.

relic chamber
Chamber situated in the middle of the stupa containing relics of the Buddha or a Buddhist Saint.

salapatala terrace
The stone-paved terrace surrounding a stupa.

samadhi
State of concentration induced by meditation.

samsara
The chain of re-birth.

sannipatasala
The hall in which the business matters of a monastery are conducted.

Sat sati
The seven half-weeks that the Buddha passed through soon after his enlightenment.

savigha
Buddhist canonical council.

savikka, or savikha
Conch-shell.

sitala maligava
A pleasure pavilion surrounded by water for coolness.

Skanda/Kataragama
The Hindu god Skanda, the son of Siva. Usually represented in Sri Lanka as the god of Kataragama, one of the most important religious centres in the island, and sacred to both Buddhists and Hindus.

stupa
A dome-shaped monument with shining sacred relics in its centre.

svastika
Symbol.

thera
A Buddhist monk.

Tooth Relic
A tooth relic of the Buddha, venerated on the Kandy Tooth Temple.

upasampada
Buddhist chapter house.

vahalkada
The elaborate altarpieces or frontispieces adjacent to the stupas and facing the four cardinal directions.

vatalage
A circular stupa house with a roof.

vana durga
'Forest barrier', e.g., a thorn fence.

vehera
Stupa.

velimalura
The sand-court below the stone terrace of a stupa.

vihara
Buddhist monastery.

Vijju kumari
'Lightning princesses'. The personification of lightning.

Bibliography

ABAYASINGHA, P.M.P. *Udarata Vitti*. Maharagama, Saman Printers, 1957.

ABAYSINGHE, T.; DEVARAJA, L.S.; SOMARATNA. *Udarata Rajadhanaya*. Colombo, Lakehouse Investments Corporation, 1977.

BANDARANAYAKE, S. *Sinhalese Monastic Architecture*. Leiden, Brill, 1974.

BANDARANAYAKE, S. *Sigiriya Project. First Archaeological Excavation Report (January-September 1982)*. Colombo, Central Cultural Fund, Ministry of Cultural Affairs, 1984.

BANDARANAYAKE, S. *The Rock and Wall Paintings of Sri Lanka*. Colombo, Lake House Bookshop, 1986.

BANDARANAYAKE, S.; MOGREN, M.; Epitawate (eds.). *The Settlement Archaeology of the Sigiriya-Dambulla Region*. Colombo, Postgraduate Institute of Archaeology, 1990.

BANDARANAYAKE, S.; DEWARAJA, L.; SILVA, R.; Wimalaratne (eds.). *Sri Lanka and the Silk Road of the Sea*. Colombo, Sri Lankan National Commission for UNESCO and Central Cultural Fund, 1990.

BASNAYAKE, H.T. *Dambulla Project: First Excavation and Research Report (April-December 1988)*. Colombo, Central Cultural Fund, Ministry of Cultural Affairs, 1989.

BASNAYAKE, H.T. *Nilangama Tudapata*, pp. 110-118. Ed.

BELL, H.C.P. *Archaeological Survey of Ceylon. Annual Report 1898*. Colombo, Government Printing Press, 1904.

CASPARIS, J.E. New Evidence on Cultural Relations between Java and Ceylon in Ancient Times. In Artibus Asiae, a *Felicitation Volume to Prof. G. Coedes*. Colombo, 1961.

CHUTIWONGS, N.; PREMATILAKA, L.; SILVA, R. *Paintings of Sri Lanka, Dambulla*, Colombo, Central Cultural Fund, Ministry of Cultural Affairs, 1990.

CHUTIWONGS, N.; PREMATILAKA, L.; SILVA, R. *Paintings of Sri Lanka, Sigiriya*, Colombo, Central Cultural Fund, Ministry of Cultural Affairs, 1990.

CODRINGTON, H.W. *Notes on the Kandyan Dynasty in the Fifteenth Century*. Ceylon Literary Register, Vol. II. Wellawatta, Wesley Press.

CODRINGTON, H.W. *A Short History of Ceylon*. London, 1947. London, Macmillan and Co., Ltd, 1947.

COOMARASWAMY, Ananda. *Medieval Sinhalese Art*. New York, Pantheon Books, 1956.

DAVY, John. *An Account of the Interior of Ceylon and its Inhabitants with Travels in that Island*. London, Longman, Hurst, Rees Orme and Brown. Paternoster Row, 1821.

DE SILVA, T.K.N.P. *The Temple of the Tooth, Kandy*. Colombo, Central Cultural Fund, Ministry of Cultural Affairs, 1985.

DE SILVA, T.K.N.P. *Kandy*. Colombo, Central Cultural Fund, Ministry of Cultural Affairs, 1988.

DEVARAJA, L.S. *Kandyan Kingdom, 1707-1760*. Colombo, 1972.

DOLAPIHILLA, P. *The Days of Sri Wickramasinghe, Last King of Kandy*. Colombo, 1959.

D'OYLEY, J. *A Sketch of the Constitution of the Great Island of Ceylon*. Dehiwala, Phillipus Baldaeus, Dutugamunu Street, 1950.

FA-HSIEN. A Record of the Buddhist Countries. Translated from the Chinese by Li-yung-hsi. Peking, 1957.

GEIGER, Wilhelm (trans.) Culavamsa, Parts 1 and 2. Oxford University Press, Amen House, Warwick Square, 1929.

GEIGER, W.; RICKMERS (trans.) *The Culavamsa, being the More Recent Part of the Mahavamsa*. Colombo, Ceylon Government Information Department, 1953.

GEIGER, W.; BODE, M.H. (trans.). *The Mahavamsa, or the Great Chronicle of Ceylon*. Colombo, Ceylon Government Information Department, 1960.

GODAKUMBURA, C.E. *Sinhalese Doorways*. Colombo, Archaeology Department, Sir Marcus Fernando Mawatha, 1966.

GODAKUMBURA, C.E. *Terracotta Heads*. Colombo, Archaeology Department.

GURUGE, A.W.P. *Asoka the Righteous: A Definitive Biography*, Central Cultural Fund, Colombo, 1993.

GURUGE, A.W.P. (trans.) *The Mahavamsa*. Associated Newspapers of Ceylon Ltd., Colombo, 1991.

GURUGE, A.W.P. *Voices from Ancient Sri Lanka*. Ministry of Cultural Affairs, Colombo, 1990.

HOCART, A.M. *The Temple of the Tooth Relic*. Memoirs of the Archaeological Survey of Ceylon, Vol. IV. London, Messrs. Luzac & Company, 1931.

JONVILLE, M. *MacDowell's Embassy of 1800*. Journal of the Royal Asiatic Society, Vol. XXXVIII, pt. 1, 1948.

KARUNARATNA, L.K. *Wooden Architecture of Sri Lanka*. Ceylon Historical Journal, Vol. XXV, No. 1-4. Dehiwala, Thisara Dutugamunu Street, 1978.

KARUNATILAKA, A.P.D. *Senkadagalapura Itihasaya*. Kandy, 1955.

KNOX, Robert. *An Historical Relation of Ceylon*. London, Chiswell, Printer to the Royal Society, St. Paul's Churchyard, 1681.

LOURIE, A.C. Gazetteer of the Central Province, Vol. I and II. Colombo, George Skeen, Government Printer, 1896, 1898.

LUDOWYK, E.F.C. (ed.) *Robert Knox in the Kandyan Kingdom*. Oxford, Oxford University Press, 1948.

NANDASIRI, Henepola, *Malwattu Maha Vihara Prabhavaya*. Unpublished M.A. Thesis, Vidyodaya Campus, 1978.

NANAYAKKARA, Wesak. *Return to Kandy*. Colombo, Arasan Printers, 30, Hyde Park Corner, 1971.

PARANAVITANA, S. *Sigiri Graffiti, being Sinhalese Verses of the Eighth, Ninth and Tenth Centuries. 2* vols. London, Oxford University Press (for the Government of Ceylon), 1956.

PEIRIS, Ralph. *Kandyan Kingdom, Political and Administrative Structure at the British Accession*. Colombo, (unpublished).

PERCIVAL, Robert. *An Account of the Island of Ceylon*. London, C. and R. Baldwin, New Bridge Street, Blackfriers, 1805.

RATNAYAKE, H.A. *Jetavanarama Research Report; First Archaeological Excavation and Research Report (January–June 1982)*. Colombo, Central Cultural Fund, Ministry of Cultural Affairs, 1984.

RAY, H.C.; PARANAVITANA, S. *History of Ceylon – Ceylon University Edition*, Vol. I, pts. 1 and 2. Colombo, Ceylon University Press, 1959, 1960.

ROHANADHEERA, Mendis (ed.) *Asgiriya Talpata*. Colombo, Sri Lanka Vidyodaya University Printing Press, Vidyodaya, 1960.

ROWLAND, B. *The Wall-paintings of India Central India and Ceylon*. Boston, Merrymount Press. 1938 Reprint Delhi Publications, 1985.

SENAVIRATNE, A. *Golden Rock Temple of Dambulla; Caves of Infinite Buddhas*. Colombo, Central Cultural Fund, Ministry of Cultural Affairs, 1983.

SILVA, R. *Religious Architecture in Early and Medieval Sri Lanka, a study*. Leiden, Brill, 1988.

STILL, J. *Ancient Capitals of Ceylon*, Colombo, H.W. Cave, 1907.

SURATH WICKRAMASINGHE ASSOCIATION. *Abhayagiri Vihara Project; First Architectural Conservation Report, 1981*. Colombo, Central Cultural Fund, 1989.

TAKAFUSU ed. *Taisho Tripitake*, Vol. 50. Tokyo, 1927.

TURNER, L.J.B. *A Description of the Town of Kandy about the Year 1815 A.D.* Ceylon Antiquary, Vol. IV, No. 2. Colombo, Times of Ceylon, 1918.

VACHISSARA, Kotagama. *Saranankara Sangharaja Samaya*. Colombo, Y. Don Alwin & Co., 1964.

VEPAGODA, Thera Amaramoli, ed. *Nikayasangraha*. Colombo, 1955.

VON SCHROEDER, Ulrik. *The Golden Age of Bronzes in Sri Lanka*. Hongkong, 1992.

WICKRAMASINGHE. Don Martion de Silva Epigraphic, Vol I. Colombo, Archaeological Survey of Ceylon, 1912. Reprinted Government of Sri Lanka 1976.

WICKRAMAGE, C. *Abhayagiri Vihara Project; First Report of the Archaeological Excavation at the Abhayagiri Vihara Complex (September 1981-April 1982)*. Colombo, 1984.

Index

Credits and Acknowledgements

It is necessary to place on record the efforts made by the Director General of UNESCO and his staff in the Cultural Division who worked closely with the Central Cultural Fund and its staff to produce this volume entitled "The Cultural Triangle of Sri Lanka". Both UNESCO and Sri Lanka relied heavily on the best professionals in the field of culture and book production, the results of which are expressed in this valuable publication.

The initiative to have a book written on the Cultural Triangle of Sri Lanka was made by UNESCO, utilizing the resources made available to it from the contributions of Member States to the Cultural Triangle. This idea was twinned with the need for a second campaign on behalf of the UNESCO/Sri Lanka Project. With the proposal accepted, UNESCO sent out Mr. Barry Lane to work with the Sri Lankan colleagues handling the six sub projects of the Cultural Triangle. Mr. Barry Lane's efforts were greatly relieved with the collaboration he obtained from Mr. Albert Dharmasiri, a professional graphic artist who has worked closely with the Cultural Triangle on many other publications. This team worked with the directors of the UNESCO/Sri Lanka Project and the authors under the Chairman of the Editorial Committee.

The written material, was in many ways, the research of the authors themselves, The photographers of these projects and other colleagues contributed the exceptional photographs. The drawings of the monuments and sites of the Cultural Triangle were executed with professional finesse to achieve the necessary international standards. Both photographers and draughtsmen are acknowledged below.

Credit should be given to the managers who exercised their professionalism to produce a book of this nature to such high standards and with in an exceptionally short period, of six months. In this regard Mr. H.D.S. Hettipathirana, Mr. H.S. de Silva, Mrs. Gnana Maldeniya, and Mr. G. Ratnasiri should be congratulated.

It should also be noted that the personnel at Lazerprint and the officers of Aitken Spence have provided their professional services with love and dedication.

Credit is also due to those who supplied material for the book in the form of Lake House Book Shop with some photographs, the Postgradute Institute of Archaeology, the Department of Archaeology and Gamma of Paris for their co-operation and assistance.

The Editorial Committee wishes to place on record the contributors of photographs and drawings.

Photo Credits:– The numbers refer to the pages – Athula Amarasekera: 54 (top); Ravilal Anthonis: 127; Senake Bandaranayake: 125, 128 (bottom), 135; Nihal Fernando: 33, 87; GAMMA/Patrimoine 2001/Robert Polidori, France: Cover: 52, 54 (bottom), 74-75, 88-89, 93, 94-95, 101, 103 (top), 131, 136, 144, 129; R. Jayasekera – CCF: 31, 39, 59, 67 (bottom), 69, 71, 77, 80, 82, 83, 84, 98 104, 105, 110, 160, 167, 172; G. Jayasinghe (Lake .House Book Shop): 117, 118, 142-143, 146, 147, 148-149, 150, 151 (top); L. K. Karunaratne: 106, 107 (bottom); M. W. E. Karunaratna: 186-187; Barry Lane: 42, 44-45, 53,55,56,57,58,64, 67 (top), 70,79, 156, 165; I. S. Madanayake – PGIAR: 138, 139, 145, 153, 154, 155, 167; L. G. Manavadu – CCF: 151ˆ(bottom), 152; C. Purankumbura – CCF: 164, 169, 170, 171,175; R. Swathe (Inc): 113, 132, 133, 134; Upali Upananda – CCF: 119, 120, 121, 123, 126, 128, 130; Jayantha Wijewardena: 49, 51, 60, 61, 62; Library Pictures: 24, 63, 81, 97, 99, 102, 103 (bottom), 107 (top), 109, 124, 155, 161, 173, 174.

Drawing credits:– Central Cultural Fund, KAVA and PGIAR (137) Suchith Mohotti Associates